MACMILLAN MASTER GUIDES

MASTER GUIDES

GENERAL EDITOR: JAMES GIBSON

JANE AUSTEN	*Emma* Norman Page
	Sense and Sensibility Judy Simons
	Persuasion Judy Simons
	Pride and Prejudice Raymond Wilson

CHARLOTTE BRONTË	*Jane Eyre* Robe
EMILY BRONTË	*Wuthering Heig*
JOHN BUNYAN	*The Pilgrim's Pr*
GEOFFREY CHAUCER	*The Miller's Tale* Michael Alexander
	The Pardoner's Tale Geoffrey Lester
	The Wife of Bath's Tale Nicholas Marsh
	The Knight's Tale Anne Samson
	The Prologue to the Canterbury Tales
	Nigel Thomas and Richard Swan
JOSEPH CONRAD	*The Secret Agent* Andrew Mayne
CHARLES DICKENS	*Bleak House* Dennis Butts
	Great Expectations Dennis Butts
	Hard Times Norman Page
GEORGE ELIOT	*Middlemarch* Graham Handley
	Silas Marner Graham Handley
	The Mill on the Floss Helen Wheeler
T. S. ELIOT	*Murder in the Cathedral* Paul Lapworth
	Selected Poems Andrew Swarbrick
HENRY FIELDING	*Joseph Andrews* Trevor Johnson
E. M. FORSTER	*A Passage to India* Hilda D. Spear
	Howards End Ian Milligan
WILLIAM GOLDING	*The Spire* Rosemary Sumner
	Lord of the Flies Raymond Wilson
OLIVER GOLDSMITH	*She Stoops to Conquer* Paul Ranger
THOMAS HARDY	*The Mayor of Casterbridge* Ray Evans
	Tess of the d'Urbervilles James Gibson
	Far from the Madding Crowd
	Colin Temblett-Wood
BEN JONSON	*Volpone* Michael Stout
JOHN KEATS	*Selected Poems* John Garrett
RUDYARD KIPLING	*Kim* Leonée Ormond
PHILIP LARKIN	*The Less Deceived* and *The Whitsun Weddings*
	Andrew Swarbrick

MACMILLAN MASTER GUIDES

D.H. LAWRENCE	*Sons and Lovers* R. P. Draper
HARPER LEE	*To Kill a Mockingbird* Jean Armstrong
LAURIE LEE	*Cider with Rosie* Brian Tarbitt
GERARD MANLEY HOPKINS	*Selected Poems* R. J. C. Watt
CHRISTOPHER MARLOWE	*Doctor Faustus* David A. Male
THE METAPHYSICAL POETS	Joan van Emden
THOMAS MIDDLETON and WILLIAM ROWLEY	*The Changeling* Tony Bromham
ARTHUR MILLER	*The Crucible* Leonard Smith
	Death of a Salesman Peter Spalding
GEORGE ORWELL	*Animal Farm* Jean Armstrong
WILLIAM SHAKESPEARE	*Richard II* Charles Barber
	Othello Tony Bromham
	Hamlet Jean Brooks
	King Lear Francis Casey
	Henry V Peter Davison
	The Winter's Tale Diana Devlin
	Julius Caesar David Elloway
	Macbeth David Elloway
	The Merchant of Venice A. M. Kinghorn
	Measure for Measure Mark Lilly
	Henry IV Part I Helen Morris
	Romeo and Juliet Helen Morris
	A Midsummer Night's Dream Kenneth Pickering
	The Tempest Kenneth Pickering
	Coriolanus Gordon Williams
	Antony and Cleopatra Martin Wine
	Twelfth Night R. P. Draper
GEORGE BERNARD SHAW	*St Joan* Leonée Ormond
RICHARD SHERIDAN	*The School for Scandal* Paul Ranger
	The Rivals Jeremy Rowe
ALFRED TENNYSON	*In Memoriam* Richard Gill
EDWARD THOMAS	*Selected Poems* Gerald Roberts
ANTHONY TROLLOPE	*Barchester Towers* K. M. Newton
JOHN WEBSTER	*The White Devil* and *The Duchess of Malfi* David A. Male
VIRGINIA WOOLF	*To the Lighthouse* John Mepham
	Mrs Dalloway Julian Pattison
WILLIAM WORDSWORTH	*The Prelude Books I and II* Helen Wheeler

MACMILLAN MASTER GUIDES

JANE EYRE

BY CHARLOTTE BRONTË

ROBERT MILES

MACMILLAN

First published 1988 by
THE MACMILLAN PRESS LTD
Houndmills, Basingstoke, Hampshire RG21 2XS
and London
Companies and representatives
throughout the world

ISBN 0–333–43409–9

A catalogue record for this book is available
from the British Library.

Printed in Hong Kong

Reprinted 1992

CONTENTS

GENERAL EDITOR'S PREFACE

The aim of the Macmillan Master Guides is to help you to appreciate the book you are studying by providing information about it and by suggesting ways of reading and thinking about it which will lead to a fuller understanding. The section on the writer's life and background has been designed to illustrate those aspects of the writer's life which have influenced the work, and to place it in its personal and literary context. The summaries and critical commentary are of special importance in that each brief summary of the action is followed by an examination of the significant critical points. The space which might have been given to repetitive explanatory notes has been devoted to a detailed analysis of the kind of passage which might confront you in an examination. Literary criticism is concerned with both the broader aspects of the work being studied and with its detail. The ideas which meet us in reading a great work of literature, and their relevance to us today, are an essential part of our study, and our Guides look at the thought of their subject in some detail. But just as essential is the craft with which the writer has constructed his work of art, and this may be considered under several technical headings — characterisation, language, style and stagecraft, for example.

The authors of these Guides are all teachers and writers of wide experience, and they have chosen to write about books they admire and know well in the belief that they can communicate their admiration to you. But you yourself must read and know intimately the book you are studying. No one can do that for you. You should see this book as a lamp-post. Use it to shed light, not to lean against. If you know your text and know what it is saying about life, and how it says it, then you will enjoy it, and there is no better way of passing an examination in literature.

JAMES GIBSON

ACKNOWLEDGEMENTS

All references to the text are taken from *Jane Eyre*, edited by Q. D. Leavis (Penguin English Library, 1966).

Cover illustration: *The Blind Girl* by John Everett Millais, courtesy of the Birmingham Museum and Art Gallery.

1 CHARLOTTE BRONTË
LIFE AND BACKGROUND

1.1 LIFE

The Brontë family grew up in Howarth, a small village perched high in the Pennines. That the daughters of an obscure clergyman in a remote part of England should produce such brilliant books as *Jane Eyre* and *Wuthering Heights* has always amazed the reading public, so much so that one can properly speak of the 'Brontë legend'. Howarth's status as the second most visited literary shrine in England indicates how potent that legend has become.

The Brontë family (five girls and a boy) arrived in Howarth in 1820. Charlotte, the third eldest, was then four. The misfortune that dogged the family struck within a year when Mrs Brontë died of cancer. Elizabeth Branwell, her sister, settled in at the parsonage to help Patrick Brontë raise his family.

Despite poor Irish beginnings, Patrick Brontë achieved considerable success; he had been to Cambridge, had published two books, and was now permanent curate of Howarth. Nevertheless, his meagre income forced him to send his daughters to the newly opened, and charitable, Clergy Daughters' School at Cowan Bridge. The choice was disastrous. The two oldest girls died within a year from tuberculosis, and Charlotte and Emily were quickly withdrawn. Charlotte was to blame the school for her sisters' deaths and her own impaired growth. The envenomed portraits of Lowood and Mr Brocklehurst appear to be Charlotte exacting revenge, for they are clearly recognisable as Cowan Bridge and its master, the Reverend Carus Wilson.

Charlotte was later sent to a more humane establishment where she eventually joined the staff. Emily and Anne found employment as governesses, Branwell as tutor. Anne adapted best, Emily not at all, while Branwell's tutorship ended in humiliating scandal when he contracted a hopeless passion for his employer's wife. In 1842 Charlotte and Emily went to Brussels in order to gain the necessary qualifications to open their own school. This too was a catastrophe. Emily was irredeemably homesick, while Charlotte fell in love with Monsieur Heger, the master of the school. Charlotte returned to Brussels a year later, to complete her studies, but by this time her secret and apparently unconfessed love had grown to unmanageable proportions. If Charlotte was unaware of the exact nature of her devotion to Monsieur Heger, Madame Heger was not, and Charlotte was ignominiously despatched before any scandal developed.

Apart from these interludes, the family unit remained largely intact, and this was especially true of the periods 1831–35, and 1845–48/9, the fatal year when Anne, Emily and Branwell successively perished from tuberculosis. The Brontë legend grows out of these periods of family unity, the Brontës displaying an astonishing creativity in spite of their relative youth, isolation and hardship.

To the eye of an outsider, the Brontës lived an uneventful, cloistered existence. The impression was even shared by Patrick Brontë, too busy with his own studying and sermon writing to notice the feverish literary activity buzzing about him. When *Jane Eyre* became the literary sensation of the season, no one was more astonished than he to discover that the celebrated Currer Bell was his own daughter, the obvious quality of the novel doubling the shock. The first period of family unity was perhaps the most crucial to the Brontë history, for it was at this time that the children began to spin their mythical kingdoms, Charlotte and Branwell developing Angria, Emily and Anne, Gondal.

The stories of Gondal and Angria were initially plays built around a box of soldiers belonging to Branwell. They soon grew into immense epics which the children wrote down, painstakingly, in miniscule, home-made books. Charlotte destroyed the Gondal saga on Emily's death, but Angria survives. As one might expect, the stories are tinged with fantasy, being set in remote, fabulous places, with larger-than-life heroes and beautiful heroines. There is swashbuckling in the Byronic manner, but there is also a love interest, with the central Duke of Zamorna having a wife and several mistresses. At this stage it is impossible to tell whether their style of romantic writing derived from an adolescent aptitude for fantasy, or from their reading. Too poor to buy new books, they depended on the rather indifferent lending libraries of the towns close to them, which left them ignorant of contemporary writing, but well versed in Byron (1788–1824), Scott (1771–1832) and oriental tales. The early Brontë sagas left a mark on their later works, especially in their strange, gothic and impenetrably ambivalent aspects. The second period of family unity marked the turning point of their literary careers. At Charlotte's urging they collected their poetry in one volume, which was produced at their own expense under the sexually misleading pen names of Currer, Ellis and Acton Bell. Emboldened by the project, they embarked on novel writing, Anne producing *Agnes Grey*, Emily *Wuthering Heights* (both 1847), and Charlotte, using her Brussels experience, *The Professor*. Anne and Emily's works finally found a publisher, but Charlotte's did not. Encouraged by a publisher's favourable letter, Charlotte submitted a new novel, *Jane Eyre* (1847). It was accepted, and immediately acclaimed.

Charlotte's joy was short-lived, as her remaining siblings perished. Drawing on her immense personal courage, Charlotte rallied to write *Shirley* (1849), and then *Villette* (1853), novels which still bore her idiosyncratic stamp, although more in the contemporary manner. In 1854 she married the Reverend Arthur Nicholls, her father's curate. Patrick Brontë had violently opposed his daughter's marriage, fearful that at such a late age marriage would prove fatal, fears tragically justified by Charlotte's death, of a complicated pregnancy, in 1855.

1.2 BACKGROUND

The mythical aspects of the Brontë upbringing – the astonishing creativity in spite of remoteness and hardship – can easily mislead one into believing *Jane Eyre* to be a sprig of genius with no discernible roots in the present. But one should be careful of underestimating Charlotte Brontë's interest in her time, and this is particularly true of three contemporary issues with which the novel engages: political unrest, religious controversy, and the lot of poor middle-class women. The first was inescapable, the second a part of her family life, and the third she knew directly from experience. In many respects the novel is deeply rooted in its time, which is one of its principal strengths.

The 1830s and 1840s were decades of intense political questioning. The Industrial Revolution was a primary source for social unrest. The enclosure laws of the previous century had displaced the peasantry from the land, thus creating a surplus pool of labour. To make matters worse, the period coincided with famine in Ireland. This spurred a large influx of labourers, further depressing the level of wages. In the words of the Scottish writer and critic Thomas Carlyle (1795–1881), the Irish brought the price of labour down to the equivalent of 'thirty weeks of third-rate potatoes', the going rate in Ireland.

However, the burning question was not the level of wages or unemployment, but the political one of power. The 'Condition of England' novels written at around this time – prominent examples include Disraeli's *Sybil* (1845), Mrs Gaskell's *North and South* (1854–5) and Dickens' *Hard Times* (1854) – evinced a lively concern for the parlous circumstances of the northern industrial poor while also revealing how pressing a topic poverty was. Even so, these were novels by 'middle-class' writers – the term is used loosely here – and their approach was oblique, and split by ambivalence. They deplored the lot of the poor, but found a radical shake-up of the political status quo terrifying. These novelists were humanely concerned, but the task of confronting the root cause of unrest was extremely trying.

Carlyle's wonderfully informative essay, 'Chartism' (1839), from which the quotation on Irish wages is taken, provides a very vivid picture of this unrest. Carlyle's response of sympathetic horror is also fascinating, and perhaps instructive. Chartism was a working-class movement active between the years 1837 and 1848. Commanding widespread support, it arose as a response to the shortcomings of the Reform Bill of 1832, which had only marginally increased the numbers of those entitled to vote. The bill retained a property qualification which excluded the working class from the political process, and hence from power. The six points of the 'People's Charter', hence 'Chartism', sought to remedy this by removing the property qualification and extending the vote to all adult males. Carlyle sympathised with the economic grievances that lay behind Chartism, but he could not accept the political demands inspiring it, which he interpreted as 'Bellowings, *in*articulate cries as of a dumb creature in rage and pain'. Poverty and exclusion from the political process were deep causes of working-class unrest. Sympathising with poverty was one thing; accepting that power should be conceded was quite another.

These issues would have been unavoidable almost anywhere in Britain, and Howarth, which had both mills and unrest, was no exception. In *Jane Eyre*, Charlotte Brontë touches upon these explosive political issues, indirectly yet powerfully. That she touched a raw nerve seems evident from the reactions of the establishment journals. *The Christian Remembrancer* claimed that 'Every page burns with moral Jacobinism' (Jacobins being supporters of the French Revolution). The *Quarterly Review*, going one better, called the novel's cast of mind the same as that 'which has overthrown authority and violated every code human and divine abroad, and fostered Chartism and rebellion at home'. What these writers have in mind is Jane's insistence that she is as good as her social betters, which carries with it the radical implication that the arrangements of social privilege are unjust. This 'moral Jacobinism', however, is closely enmeshed with the novel's religious references, an understandable connection as religion was sometimes used as an instrument of power.

The issue of the 'political' abuse of religion is best approached from the point of view of those who suffer from it, which is how the novel approaches it. The girls of the Lowood school are the hapless victims of a religious institution, and again it was economic circumstances that put them there. As the contemporary French critic Eugène Forçade put it, it is from the 'needy middle class' that Charlotte Brontë chooses her heroine. Forçade notes that in England the old order of primogeniture still exists – the practice of the oldest son inheriting everything – and as a result the 'aristocracy still offers up its own children to the sacrifice of poverty' in order to keep the family line and property intact. The oldest son would inherit the bulk of the wealth, leaving the other siblings to seek their living among the professions. As with the aristocracy, so with the middle class, and in the case of women the matter was much worse as professions were fewer. As a result they were 'sacrificed to poverty' in order not to split the family wealth, just as Mrs Reed's would have been if she had accepted Jane within the family circle. Lowood's regime of renunciation thus becomes eloquent. As 'surplus female relations', the girls at Lowood are schooled in both obedience and the accomplishments required of the two very dismal occupations open to them, that of teacher and governess. Marriage offers the only real means of recouping their position, an uncertain prospect without beauty or money.

Self-sacrifice does not come naturally, so it is the business of Lowood to enforce it. It does so by drawing on the authority of religion, exceedingly diverse at this time, but one can make a rudimentary sense of its divisions by noting that they roughly follow class lines. The Church of England had its roots in the landed gentry, while the working poor favoured Dissent, particularly Methodism, which grew out of the Evangelical movement founded by John Wesley (1707–88). Although directed at the poor, Methodism was initially middle class in inspiration. John Wesley did not want to break with the Church of England, but was forced to do so when it refused to ordain his movement's priests, who were much in demand among the poor. The 'livings' of the established Church, that is to say posts as ministers, were much sought after by the younger sons of the gentry, and naturally enough such men had little in common with the urban poor. A void was created in the latter's religious needs, which Methodism filled.

But Methodism was only one branch of a larger Evangelical movement (for the basic tenets of Evangelicism, see Section 3.3 below). There was also a less radical, middle-class strand of Evangelicism which did not break with the Church of England. The novel examines this strand. The moral welfare of the poor was the ostensible concern of this middle-class Evangelicism, but whether it really helped the poor remained doubtful. It offered spiritual solutions to material problems while giving moral support to a political system in which the poor did very badly. In this respect it is arguable that religion was used as an instrument of social power, an argument that will be looked at in greater detail in the sections below.

Political unrest, religious controversy and the lot of poor middle-class women are all drawn together by a single thread, the individual's protest against a repressive society. In the figure of Jane Eyre, the struggle against political, religious and sexual repression are brought together. In gaining the measure of the book's rebelliousness it is therefore necessary to keep in mind the sensitivity that surrounded these issues, and the difficulty of going against the grain of many deep-seated social prejudices.

2 SUMMARIES

AND

CRITICAL COMMENTARY

2.2 OVERALL SUMMARY OF THE PLOT

Jane Eyre is the story of an orphan told in her own words. The narrative is revealed retrospectively and chronologically. From the vantage point of the present Jane Eyre looks back into the past, revealing the significant events of her life more or less in the order in which they happened. Even so, although the sequence of her history is not tampered with, there are omissions. Some chapters cover hours, others years.

For the purposes of discussion critics divide narrative into 'plot' and 'history'. By 'history' they mean the order in which the events happened, by 'plot' the order in which they are told. For example, detective fiction is frequently told 'backwards', in that the events that start the story going (the exact details of the crime) are only fully disclosed at the end. Such a mismatch of plot and history makes for a suspenseful, complicated narrative. *Jane Eyre*, by way of contrast, is an uncomplicated narrative in that plot and history are relatively congruent. One can gain an idea of how apparently simple it is by comparing it with Emily Brontë's *Wuthering Heights*, with its 'Chinese box' technique of narratives within narratives and its highly evolved time scheme.

As we shall see, the narrative technique of *Jane Eyre* is not as simple as this makes it seem, but it is by and large true to say that the novel's complexities arise from plotting. In a famous definition of plot, E. M. Forster said that with 'the king died and then the queen died', you have a story but not a plot, but with 'the king died, and then the queen died of grief', you have a story and a plot. Forster's point is that for plots to thicken you need 'causality' or motive. One way of describing the act of interpreting *Jane Eyre* is to say that it is about the discovery of motives, of attributing a psychology to the principal characters, but especially to Jane, that would make sense of the causality of events. The book is full of hints as to possible motives, but it is the reader who pieces them together. In the following section we will be investigating these hints and the complications of plotting that they suggest. This will prepare us for the next section on themes which are evolved from the plot.

Overall the plot is as follows. Being an orphan, Jane is dependent upon her Aunt Reed who is the widow of her mother's brother. There is no blood tie between Jane and her aunt, and in addition she carries the burden of her mother's bad marriage to a penniless clergyman. In Mrs Reed's eyes, this is a blot on the family name. Jane does not act decorously, given her lowly, disgraced station, and Mrs Reed rids the family of its embarrassing encumbrance by sending Jane to Mr Brocklehurst's boarding-school, a 'charitable' institution for orphans, the daughters of poor clergymen and other girls of the middle class fallen on hard times. Mrs Reed's parting shot is to brand Jane as an incorrigible liar, and once at the school Jane is publically humiliated by Mr Brocklehurst for this defect. The experience has its benefits, however, for through it Jane makes two important friends, Miss Temple and Helen Burns, who figure centrally in Jane's development. Under Mr Brocklehurst's administration the regime at the school is very harsh, so much so that many of the girls perish under it, including Helen Burns. An investigation is conducted. Conditions improve, and as she grows older Jane begins to follow in Miss Temple's footsteps as a teacher in the school. But ambitious to see more of life, and to gain greater independence, she seeks a post as a governess, and this she duly finds with Mr Rochester at Thornfield. Her charge is a young French girl who may be Rochester's illegitimate daughter, the result of his philanderings in Paris. Jane and Rochester fall in love and determine to marry despite the inequality of status, but on the day of their nuptials the existence of Rochester's mad wife is discovered by the sudden arrival of her brother. Rochester refuses to sustain this blow to his happiness and proposes to make Jane his mistress. Jane balks at this, and flies in the night. After much wandering, and in a forlorn state, she throws herself upon the mercy of a family she spies through a cottage window (two unmarried women and a clergyman). By a stroke of good fortune they turn out to be Jane's cousins, the children of her father's sister. The discovery is made due to the death of Jane's uncle in Madeira, a wealthy wine merchant. In flying from Rochester Jane has assumed an alias, but St John unravels the mystery. The Rivers children have been disinherited by their uncle who had quarrelled with their father, but Jane justly divides the legacy with her new-found cousins. St John proposes to Jane that they go as man and wife to India to do missionary work, and Jane is on the verge of accepting when the supernatural intervenes in the shape of a mysterious cry from Rochester. Jane flies to his rescue, discovering her former master in a blind and broken state in Ferndean, another of his estates. Thornfield has been burnt down by Mrs Rochester who died in the conflagration, and Rochester's injuries have been sustained through his fruitless attempts to rescue her. The way having been cleared of all impediments, the two marry, and the book ends happily.

2.2 CHAPTER SUMMARIES AND COMMENTARY

Chapter 1

Jane Eyre, we quickly learn, is an outsider. Banished from the Reed family's cosy domestic scene for an unspecified offence, she takes refuge in the breakfast room, in a window-seat, and here she reads a book, Bewick's *History of British Birds*. She is discovered by John Reed, who torments her with ugly faces, references to her dependent status, and a blow from her own book. Jane flies into a passion, and John Reed is saved only by the intervention of his mother.

Commentary
The story begins in mid-action, and as it is told in the first person, it is left to the reader to make the details fit. We discover that Jane is of physically inferior stature and, according to Mrs Reed, badly behaved, an accusation potentially undercut by the absence of a precise charge and the disproportionate punishment. A fairy tale element runs throughout the chapter, with Jane as a Cinderella figure put upon by a wicked 'stepmother' and her indulged children. The most significant, but inferential, details concern Jane's window retreat and the perusal of her book. The pictures are variations on the themes of guilt and desolation, but the scene also implies that Jane has a sensitive, if brooding, imagination. The window-seat with its red curtains underscores her alienation from the family, but it also suggests a private space, the interior of a mind, so in a very economical way the major themes and techniques of the novel are foreshadowed. A recurring structure of many narratives is loss and regain, so the concentration on loss of family here may imply an eventual regain. Such restorations are generally accompanied by an education or growth of the self, a thematic pattern into which *Jane*

Eyre apparently falls. The Cinderella element, moreover, implies a degree of self-pity, of subjective exaggeration, and it is this which gives rise to several key technical features of the narrative. In so far as the story is concerned with the growth of self, its deep realm of feelings and desires, a *symbolic* method is required where feelings find their equivalents in imagery, hence Bewick's book with its elusive pictures. But as the story is subjective – and possibly highly coloured in its recollection – it may also be misleading, and so the reader must be on guard. Both these features require the reader to participate closely in the 'construction' of the story.

Chapter 2

Having been pulled off John Reed in a violent temper, Jane is banished to the 'red-room' where she mulls over the iniquities done to her by the Reed household. We learn that Mr Reed had died in the room nine years earlier, his dying wish being that Mrs Reed should raise Jane as 'one of her own children'. Jane has the fantasy that Mr Reed's ghost might appear and offer solace, but the idea terrifies her. She mistakes a light for the ghost and screams, bringing the servants, and eventually Mrs Reed, who rebukes her for scheming. She is locked up again, and this time she faints.

Commentary
There are a number of developments here of considerable critical importance. The first concerns the retrospective paragraph beginning 'What a consternation of soul was mine that dreary afternoon!' At this point the adult stands back from the events, raising the question of whether it was right for her to have resisted through anger. The child is filled with righteous indignation at the injuries done to her, but the adult's, 'Yet in what darkness, what dense ignorance, was the mental battle fought!', is highly suggestive of the needs of Christian forbearance, virtues the young Jane has yet to learn. There is something heathen in Jane's unremitting anger, but this raises the question of what Jane's true self is, the angry child she is, or the socialised adult she may yet become? This questioning of identity is enforced in several ways. The servants' reprovals of her for troubling her benefactors raises the issue of social status. Is her social identity to be found among the class of dependants (such as the servants), or is it to be drawn from that of the family that excludes her? The answer may have a bearing on the justification of her rebelliousness. But there is also a sexual dimension that cuts across class, as both types of social identity repress female sexuality.

Two aspects of sexual repression concern us here, one general, the other specific. As night falls, Jane's spirits flag: 'My habitual mood of humiliation, self-doubt, forlorn depression, fell damp on the embers of my decaying ire.' The pun on Eyre/air/ire points to Jane's double aspect, as a creature of ire, associated with fire, anger and passion, but also as a creature of air, a light and dancing spirit. This lighter aspect is brought out by the episode where she gazes in the mirror and sees her image transformed, a 'half fairy, half imp' associated with the 'ferny dells in the moors'. At the same time the image 'specks' and 'glitters' in the glass, suggesting a residual passion, or sparking. One way of viewing Jane's development is that it represents a striving towards a balance between these two aspects, of fire and air, of passion and 'spirit', imp and fairy. In the meantime, however, obstacles are thrown in her way. Society, in the shape of the Reed household, urges conformity, or a generalised repression of her feelings and desires. To behave, to be a 'good' little girl, is to be stifled.

But along with this generalised sexual repression – the decorous behaviour society demands of all little boys and girls, but especially dependent ones – there is sexual repression in the specific sense, although this is only hinted at in ambiguous terms. The red-room is a place of mystery, partly owing to the awful aura of death. No one goes into the room except the maid who dusts it once a week, and Mrs Reed at more distant intervals to inspect 'a certain drawer in the wardrobe, where were stored diverse parchments, her jewel-casket, and a miniature of her deceased husband'. Taking their hint from the aura of mystery and prohibition, feminist critics have read this as a glancing reference to affairs of the female body. According to this view, the episode of the red-room is a rite of passage, an initiation into the mystery of female sexuality. The lavish furniture, mirrors and draperies suggest the refurbishments of a bordello, an idea given surprising backing by the female servant's threat to bind Jane with her garter, a recurring fantasy in Victorian pornography. The redness of the room, its recesses, crypts, jewel-caskets and imagery of bleeding – all these form what might be called a geography of the female body. Both enforce a contradictory lesson. In order to be a successful sexual competitor Jane must curtail her desires in order to please men's, but paradoxically her body is to be understood as an object of desire, and therefore of shame and deserved concealment (the 'initiation' must therefore occur in the awful privacy of the red-room). As a metaphorical representation of initiation, the incident suggests that for Victorian middle-class women, 'growing up' is a perverse and contradictory ordeal in which sexuality is simultaneously stressed (conforming to what appeals) and denied. Desire is something men have, but not women. Such an interpretation may offend our common-sense notion of the way literary texts express their meaning, and later on we will be looking at the grounds for such an argument. In the meantime, do you agree? If not, why not?

Chapter 3

Recovering from her faint, Jane discovers herself in the congenial care of the apothecary, Mr Lloyd. Jane draws comfort from the fact that Mr Lloyd is a stranger and not connected with the Reeds, and on a subsequent visit she divulges the origins of her unhappiness. Mr Lloyd's suggestion of a boarding-school is welcomed by Jane, a sentiment apparently shared by Mrs Reed.

Commentary
The chapter is largely digressive in that it fills in gaps from the previous two. We learn that the episode in the red-room marked an epoch in Jane's life, with her feeling the 'reverberations to this day'. The nature of this change is registered in the fate of her favourite reading matter. Hitherto *Gulliver's Travels* had been a source of unending enchantment, but now it is 'eerie and dreary', a diminishment of magic that besets children as they grow up. At the same time the reference to Swift's book foreshadows the travels Jane herself has yet to undergo. Although Jane will visit several places, the real journey is inward, a matter of personal growth. This involves a superseding of her present limitations in understanding, and one of these emerges in her talk with Mr Lloyd. Asked if she would like to live with her poor relations, she answers 'no' on the grounds of the 'degradation' of the poor. Jane is injured by class attitudes in that she is hurt but also contaminated by them. She is both victim and snob, a limitation the child will eventually overcome, or so the adult hints. Do you think she does? In the meantime the chapter sketches the uncongenial environment which makes this learning difficult. For example, Jane is ministered to by an apothecary, in itself a slight to her status, as the Reed children would have had a more costly doctor. But if poverty is a scandal, love is another, and only through eavesdropping on the servants does Jane learn the full details of her family history, the ignominy of her mother marrying for love and not cash. This prejudice is joined by another. Bessie pities Jane's deplorable history, but Abbot thinks her a 'toad'. Abbot might be sympathetic if only Jane were like Miss Georgiana, who with her

curls and blue eyes looks 'as if she were painted', which enforces the
lesson that you need only look like a doll to be treated like one.

Chapter 4

Three months pass before Mr Brocklehurst arrives to inspect Jane for
his school. Mrs Reed's accusation of deceit infuriates Jane, and once
the minister is gone Jane remonstrates passionately, and vindictively.
Disconcerted, Mrs Reed abandons the field to a now remorseful
Jane.

Commentary
The first half of the chapter is devoted to telling details. We see
Georgiana's passion for domestic play and dressing up, and the
materialistic Eliza's devotion to money. Jane has become regressive,
and comforts herself in a crib with a rag doll, or stares out at the
petrified landscape through a clear island in the frosted window, an
image of her inner state. The opening description of Mr Brocklehurst
is worth some attention:

> I looked up at – a black pillar! – such, at least, appeared to me, at
> first sight, the straight, narrow, sable-clad shape standing erect on
> the rug: the grim face at the top was like a carved mask, placed
> above the shaft by way of capital.

The figure of speech 'pillar of society' is made a joke of here, but it is
a serious joke. Mr Brocklehurst appears before his name, which has a
dehumanising effect further enforced by the imagery, which is
inexpressive, impenetrable and mineral. The figure overall is
imposing, masculine and repressive, and not at all the image of
Christian charity, which is what he is supposed to represent. The
picture he paints of life at Lowood unintentionally reveals his
hypocrisy. His own daughters are dressed in luxury, whereas the girls
at Lowood, as his daughter blurts out, are dressed 'almost like poor
people's children!' – a fact highly satisfying to both Mr Brocklehurst
and Mrs Reed. The remark unwittingly reveals the ambiguity of the
girls' status. As the indigent daughters of the middle class they are a
cut above poor people, but without money they lose their prestige.
The school is apparently charitable in that it raises and educates these
children, but its true function is not to inculcate Christian virtues, but
to use these values to disenfranchise the girls from their class, thus
instituting their loss of privilege. The use of religion as a weapon is
grotesquely revealed by Mr Brocklehurst's catechism. He asks Jane

whether she knows about the torments of hell, and leaves her with a cautionary tale of a little girl struck dead for deceit. That deceit is not the issue emerges with the comic story of Mr Brocklehurst's little boy, who professes a love of psalms, and an even greater love for ginger-bread-nuts, the rewards for his infant piety. The reader perceives him to be a little schemer, but what is charming in a moneyed boy is mortal sin in a poverty-stricken girl. Christian precepts are thus turned into instruments of class discipline: the children are schooled through religious terror to accept their deprivation.

Naturally aggrieved by Mrs Reed's accusation, Jane rebukes her with great intensity – once again she is filled with 'ire'. 'A ridge of lighted heath, alive, glancing, devouring' would have been an appropriate emblem for her mind as she 'menaced Mrs Reed', and it is this angry and defensive passion which preserves her from being quelled and defeated. However, it is also dangerous for her because it is self-destructive, an idea underlined by the black and blasted aftermath of the burnt-out heath, and the corroding after-taste of vengeance. Anger is a preservative, but not an answer.

Chapter 5

Early next morning Jane departs for Lowood, arriving safely after a long, uncomfortable journey. Jane is met by Miss Temple, who impresses her favourably. She is immediately introduced into the routine of the school. They are served burnt porridge for breakfast, but on Miss Temple's orders, bread and cheese for lunch, apparently a treat. Jane meets Helen Burns, who is subsequently made to stand in the middle of the classroom for a misdemeanour.

Commentary
The routine of the school – its 'systematic arrangements', as Helen Burns puts it – is the principal focus of the chapter. The picture that emerges is one of uncomfortable regimentation in almost every respect. The building is bitterly cold, the amenities meagre. A bell clatters at regular intervals, the girls troop to attention, learning their lessons by rote. Their dress is plain, uniform and severe, with 'not a curl visible'. As with their bodies, so with their minds. Self-expression and spontaneity are systematically discouraged.

The picture of hardship is set in ironic context by the plaque memorialising Naomi Brocklehurst's beneficence in rebuilding a portion of Lowood 'Institution'. Jane is puzzled by this word and its apparent lack of relevance to the passage of scripture that follows, a clever use of Jane's naîvete. The passage is meant to celebrate Mrs Brocklehurst's good works which will justify her before God. But in its original context 'good works' refers to spiritual rather than material manifestations of faith. The burden of the scripture (which contains the famous 'Blessed are the meek: for they shall inherit the earth') is that redemption lies in brotherly love and Christian forbearance. The ironies of 'Institution' are therefore manifold. First, it suggests regulated charity instead of the spontaneous spirit of giving; second, the institution is not there to promote the interests of the poor and meek, but to keep them that way; and third, the institution does not confer a benefit, but injures the children through its parsimony. In this respect Jane is right to question the 'connexion between the first words and the verse of Scripture', although it is left to the reader to establish the telling lack of one. To underscore the point, Jane's puzzlement is broken by the tubercular cough of Helen Burns, who will eventually die in large measure due to the un-Christian strictures of Mrs Brocklehurst's 'good works'.

Jane leaves for Lowood beneath the light of the setting moon – as we shall see, an important and recurring image. Note the contrasting nature of the description of Miss Temple. Is there any significance to be drawn from this?

Chapter 6

The next day Helen Burns is punished for her 'slatternly' habits. Her friendship with Jane grows, and the chapter ends with a conversation on theology.

Commentary
The wickedness of the school is sketched further. In a history lesson on Charles I, the girls are burdened with dry facts which only Helen Burns can answer, but instead of being rewarded she is beaten for her dirty fingernails, a reason that fills Jane with rage as the water was frozen. The simple scene is more complicated than it appears. As the chapter later makes explicitly clear, Helen Burns hold firmly to the tenets of the St Matthew scripture, and regularly turns the other cheek. So the irony of the previous chapter is deepened. The institution that alludes to the virtues of Christian forbearance draws its justification from the apparent fact that it gives its pupils ample opportunity to cultivate them. But this implicitly places the school in the role of un-Christian persecutor, a scene duly acted out with Helen Burns's flogging, which ironically mimics Christ's sufferings on Calvary. But a complication emerges with the book's rejection of

melodrama. The characters are not neatly separated into the good and the bad, malefactors and innocents. The feebleness of Miss Scatcherd's reasons for beating Helen might suggest motiveless sadism, but the reader is also free to infer a deep, impelling frustration on Miss Scatcherd's part arising from her own bleak existence in the school, so that she too is seen as a victim of an institution which not only does not merit the virtues it lays claim to, but apparently breeds the very vices it aims to extirpate. Moreover, Jane is not only shocked by the cruelty, but her own pagan and rebellious feelings are stirred up by it. Several paragraphs later the weather is used as a notation of this. The 'obscure chaos' of the weather made her 'reckless and feverish'.

The subtlety of the book's ideas develop further in the conversation with Helen, whose 'doctrine of endurance' confounds Jane. Helen's generous piety throws Jane's rebelliousness and vengeful feelings into an unfavourable light, but the book is not simply advocating forbearance. In the context of Lowood its appropriateness is questionable, and Helen's tenet of condemning the crime while excusing the criminal, although admirable in theory, has practical shortcomings. The reference to the Charles regicide is particularly deft as it raises the troublesome question of justifiable rebellion in a larger social and historical context. Helen's precepts would have ended in the bowing down before tyranny, so here Jane has the advantage. The dialectical to and fro of the argument does not encourage a conclusion, but provokes questioning and self-examination in the reader.

Chapter 7

After three weeks Mr Brocklehurst finally arrives, and it soon becomes clear that he is the principal agent of meanness in the school, even to the extent of purchasing inferior thread for the girls to sew with. Jane's worst fears are realised, and she is arraigned for deceit.

Commentary
The distresses of Lowood multiply, and with them occasions for satire. For example, the chapter opens with a description of a dog-eat-dog world in which the bigger girls rob the smaller of their meagre portions, so if the purpose of the school is to instil humility and sisterly love, it is clearly failing. And on Sundays the girls are not given the rest they sorely need, but repeat 'the Church Catechism, and the fifth, sixth and seventh chapters of St Matthew' until the

smaller ones fall down. Again, the religious references are apt.
Among other things chapter six warns against priding oneself publicly
for one's good works, while chapter seven stresses 'Judge not, that ye
be not Judged'. Mr Brocklehurst, and not the girls, would be advised
to listen.

Glaring religious hypocrisy – the disparity between professing and
doing – is one source of satire in the chapter, and another arises with
the interpolation of Jane's adult voice, which underscores it. When
Mr Brocklehurst appears he is once again the 'black column', whom
Jane refers to as 'a piece of architecture', a witticism beyond the
child's years. Again the joke conceals a serious point, which is to
identify Brocklehurst very closely with the institution: he too is stony,
buttoned up, and rigid. Another instance of retrospective satire
occurs with Jane's response to the ticking off Miss Temple receives
for substituting food for burnt porridge, as this feeds the girls' 'vile
bodies' while starving their immortal souls. Mr Brocklehurst paused,
'perhaps overcome by his feelings'. This is a very subtle knife. It
might signify the weight of his concern, or his luxuriating in self-
righteous feeling, which carries with it the unspoken irony that he
needs a stiff dose of St Matthew, chapter six. The anatomy of this
destructive institution is further revealed in the imagery of Miss
Temple's response, her face setting into the petrified severity of
marble. Even the saintly Miss Temple is in danger of becoming
marmoreal, stony and repressed. The imagery also makes Brocklehurst Medusa-like, the Gorgon which, in Greek mythology, turned
onlookers into rock, a fitting emblem for the degree of Brocklehurst's
moral hideousness. So a final irony one must keep in mind is that
however much the adult Jane stresses her emancipation from
vengeance, the interpolated satire suggests enduring bitterness.

Chapter 8

Her ordeal over, Jane melts in a flood of tears, but is then solaced by
Helen. The two girls are invited into Miss Temple's room for tea and
cakes. Telling her side of the story, Jane rebuts her accusers, and
within a week Miss Temple receives confirmation from Mr Lloyd.
Given new heart, Jane applies herself to her studies, and begins to
find happiness.

Commentary
In this chapter Jane's moral education begins to gather speed. Her
response to her humiliation is largely amoral in that she is mostly
concerned with being left 'solitary and hated'. We gain the measure

of Jane's desire to be loved from her reaction to her first taste of
domesticity – the purpose of the fire scene – which fills her with
blissful admiration. This experience of love induces a change in her.
Initially she would buy love by undergoing self-mutilating feats of
endurance, having her arm broken or being gored by a bull. Helen's
chastening 'you think too much of the love of human beings' indicates
how close to paganism Jane's attitudes are. She encourages Jane to
live in the clear light of her conscience, and with the comforting
knowledge that innocence has its certain rewards. This strengthens
Jane's reliance, and helps her live positively through the self-
cultivation of study. So rather than demanding love through self-
sacrifice, she earns it through self-improvement.

Even so, Helen's sway over Jane is revealed to be limited. As her
name suggests, and as the imagery reveals, Helen is Jane's sister in
passion, and both 'burn'. Helen tranquillises Jane, and indeed she is
associated with calm endurance. But inwardly she burns, so that the
metaphor of 'self-immolation' becomes prophetically true. Christian
forbearance, taken to Helen's extreme, is finally self-destructive.
Helen's example brings Jane considerable benefits, but Jane's difference reveals itself in the fury that 'burns' within her at Helen's
humiliation.

Chapter 9

Now springtime, the school is ironically struck down with typhus, so
while the buds of spring grow, the school's perish. The relaxed
discipline allows Jane to roam the hills. Helen is dying of tuberculosis, and Jane creeps in to visit her. She stays the night, and in the
morning Helen is dead.

Commentary
The chapter opens with the quickening of spring, and in this way the
ironic contrast is enforced. The image of hills and dales and burgeon-
ing vegetation suggests a pastoral idyll where man lives harmoniously
with nature. The fact that the school is to the contrary riddled with
disease – the 'effluvia of mortality – underlines how unnatural it is.
Jane's delight in open-air rambles befits both a normal young girl,
and a healthy young animal. Note Jane's justification for not visiting
Helen sooner. This may be an innocent explanation, or it may
indicate that Jane feels guilty for attending to nature rather than to
her friend. In this view Jane suffers an unresolved conflict between
feeling and morality.

Chapter 10

Years have passed and Jane is now a young woman of eighteen. Robbed of Miss Temple, she determines to seek her fortune, arranging a job as governess at Thornfield. Bessie's visit conveys the family news, and a contrast is drawn between the cousins' attainments, the Reed children having physical advantages, Jane moral and artistic ones. Bessie also relates a flying visit made by Jane's paternal uncle, apparently a tradesman.

Commentary
In the intervening years Jane has grown little physically, but a great deal morally. Superficially she is 'a disciplined and subdued character', her feelings 'better regulated'. But Miss Temple's departure has revealed to Jane that she is still inwardly restless. Absence has incurred a 'transforming process' in which all that her mind has 'borrowed' from Miss Temple has fallen away. Miss Temple had given her a 'motive', and without it Jane regresses, her old feelings stirring anew.

Although Jane now thinks it a good thing that she conforms to the values of the reformed Lowood – with Mr Brocklehurst's demotion it has become 'a truly useful and noble institution' – it is left to the reader to decide whether conformity is actually desirable. Has she improved morally, or is she only subdued? Is the return of her old rebellious feelings and desires a pitiable regression, or is it progressive, a reassertion of her truest self? Although Jane compliments the institution, her sole motive for staying is the disconnected one of her love for Miss Temple, which would indicate the school's incapacity to satisfy her deeper needs. Indeed, her leaving appears more in the way of an escape than a departure – witness the paragraph in which her eye longingly traverses the distance while she inwardly gasps for liberty. Her suddenly pragmatic desire for a 'new servitude' is thus highly ironic, contrasted as it is with images of the open road, her panegyric on the school, and her references to her happily regulated feelings.

Chapter 11

Jane arrives at Thornfield with the mistaken belief that Mrs Fairfax is the owner. She learns her mistake, meets Adèle, discovers a few facts about Rochester, and is given a tour of the house. A strange laugh heard in the attic is attributed to a servant, Grace Poole.

Commentary
This is a chapter of first impressions, and therefore of mysteries. Rochester is absent, but the house hints at his character. The exterior with its battlements has a 'picturesque' look, while the surrounding countryside is pastoral, idyllic, and therefore comforting. So from the outside Thornfield appears the seat of an ordinary country gentleman, but the interior suggests a different story. For example, the third-floor rooms, especially antique, are bathed in pallid moonlight, the gothic gloom further heightened by the curious effigies. The forbidding interior dispels the comforting impression conveyed by the outside, a menace increased by the rumour of the Rochesters' racial violence. The contrast between inside and outside repeats itself as Jane descends the ladder into the attic, with pastoral delight above, a black vault below. Notice, too, the earlier description of the drawing-room with its 'general blending of snow and fire'. Are these portents of Rochester's character?

The chapter abounds in further misunderstandings, contradictions and mysteries. Jane confuses Mrs Fairfax's station, there is the enigma of Adèle's background and her odd mixture of childishness and sexual precocity and, perhaps most importantly, there is Jane's troubled introspection into her natural aspirations to feminine beauty, which she can understand but not express. So while Jane's arrival is superficially smooth, there are portents of disruption and change which undermine the confident assertion that opens the next chapter.

Chapter 12

Feeling restless, Jane walks out into the lanes on a fine, cold winter's afternoon. As the sun sets, a strange dog appears followed by a horseman who takes a spill on the ice. Jane helps him remount, and returning to Thornfield discovers him to be Rochester.

Commentary
Bored by domestic life in Thornfield, Jane burns after 'bright visions'. She attends to an inner narrative, 'quickened with all of incident, life, fire and feeling, that I desired, and had not in my actual existence'. In this chapter dream becomes reality. Indeed, the prelude to Rochester's appearance is dreamy and 'romantic', as if a scene from a romance. A pale moon flickers brightly while currents of life stir unseen in the surrounding hills and dales. A horse approaches, and Jane recalls Bessie's tales of the 'Gytrash', a mythical spirit of the North that haunts the solitary ways, and indeed a strange dog-like creature glides into view, but a human presence

breaks the spell. Just as the 'Gytrash' materialises as an actual, if exotic, dog with the prosaic name of 'Pilot', so the rider materialises as something other than the 'handsome, heroic-looking young gentleman' of more conventional fiction. To the contrary, he is of medium height, somewhat swarthy, with heavy brows and an ireful look. So although the chapter hints that Jane's romantic yearnings will in fact be realised, it further hints that these yearnings will not be identical with conventional fantasy.

Chapter 13

Jane is invited to 'tea' with Rochester, who interrogates her about her past. He requests a demonstration of her piano playing and inspects her paintings. Later Jane asks after Rochester's history, but is met by Mrs Fairfax's evasive replies.

Commentary
Jane's conversation with Rochester establishes the nature of their relationship. He is brusque, peremptory and demanding, but Jane prefers this to 'finished politeness', which would disconcert her. Although she would rather observe than speak, she is not cowed by Rochester, and is pertly direct in her answers. This resistance is foreshadowed in the episode of the dress, where she rejects donning her finery, dressing to please her own sense of decorum, and not other people's. Both appear as staunch individualists, he refusing the conventions of manners, and she those of her position. Another area of similarity emerges with Rochester's history. Like her, he was sacrificed to the necessity of keeping the family money intact, and as a second son was forced into a 'painful position'. Mrs Fairfax attributes his 'changeful and abrupt' manner to this, but leaves its exact origin obscure.

Chapter 14

Several uneventful days pass until once again Jane is summoned by Rochester. In the ensuing conversation he perplexes Jane with references to his reproachable past, and mysterious plans for redemption.

Commentary
The courtship between Rochester and Jane continues, although Jane refuses to recognise it as such. However, her delight in him is evident from her description as he leans against the mantlepiece, which

radiates personal rather than bodily charm, the former being the more piquant and attractive. Phrenology – the nineteenth-century science of discovering character from cranial bumps – is used further to elaborate Rochester's personal make-up. Although clearly intellectual, his forehead is bereft of signs of 'benevolence', a deficiency offset by the protuberance indicative of conscience. Indeed, his thoughts 'are galled with dwelling on one point'; he is 'hampered, burdened, cursed'. He alludes to a mysterious being who has the power to reform him, even though accepting her requires a 'new statute' to legalise it. He is determined in this, but Jane warns against it. Rochester clearly means Jane by this redemptive being, but the class boundary separating them inhibits her thinking it. If Jane does not recognise the first moves in their courtship, the reader does, but the possible impediment to their union – the origin of Rochester's tortured conscience – is left a mystery.

Chapter 15

Intense and conflicting emotions grip Rochester as he spies the upper storeys of Thornfield while relating to Jane his sordid past with Céline Varens. Jane ponders this mystery, and then further reflects on Rochester's behaviour to her. She now expresses herself delighted with Rochester's appearance and character. Fretful, she is unable to sleep, and investigating a weird laugh she discovers Rochester alight in his bed. Jane douses the fire, while Rochester expresses profuse thanks.

Commentary
The structure of this chapter is shrewd and subtle. The episode of Adèle's dress in the previous chapter, in which she appears as the diminutive image of her mother, together with Céline's history, serve to enforce the idea that Rochester has renounced the conventional type of feminine attraction in favour of more sturdy charms, with Jane's eligibility the clear implication. But if she is fit for him, it is unclear that he is fit for her. For the unconventional Jane, the Paris adventure has left no stigma, but she does believe some 'cruel cross of fate' has left him 'spoiled and tangled'. The two developments come together in the paragraph beginning 'And was Mr Rochester now ugly in my eyes?' His recent correctness in his sexual tastes leads her to declare her interest in him – although couched in moral and detached terms – but his inner turbulence remains a problem. Jane still fails to recognise that her interest might be amorous rather than altruistic, and Rochester's mysterious look in the avenue (presu-

mably directed at his wife in the attic) gives her a sleepless night, much as if she intuitively feared a threat to her still unconscious passion. Significantly this first allusion to Jane's desire coincides with Mrs Rochester's first attack, which suggests a link. At this stage it is worth pondering what it might be. The chapter's structure, then, is that we move from what Rochester no longer likes to what he might like (Céline to Jane), and then to the obstacle preventing their union, which may be the literal impediment of Mrs Rochester, or the metaphorical one of Rochester's unfitness.

Chapter 16

Next morning Jane is perplexed to learn that Rochester has explained the fire as an innocent accident. Unable to fathom his motive for lying, she scrutinises Grace Poole for signs of guilt which she finds in Grace's accomplished *sang froid*. Speculating further, she imagines a youthful indiscretion on Rochester's part has delivered him into Grace Poole's power. Jane waits for Rochester's appearance in order to tease an explanation from him, but learns he has gone to 'the Leas', where he will undoubtedly meet the beautiful heiress, Blanche Ingram. Confronted with a rival, Jane admits her secret passion, chiding herself for her impossible and unwise ambitions.

Commentary
Charlotte Brontë's narrative technique – her use of Jane's limited point of view – allows her to lay down several false trails which increase the mystery and tension. Her suspicion of Grace Poole is one such trail, her jealousy of Blanche Ingram another. One source of Jane's limited knowledge is the uninformative and contradictory behaviour of Rochester, into which she can have no insight. But an equally important blank is the mystery of her own heart, and this makes for a very revealing ambiguity in her narrative. She scotches the notion that Grace Poole was once Rochester's mistress on the grounds of Grace's uncomely appearance, but this leads to thoughts of her own plainness, and the hitherto unadmitted belief that he favours her. That he once had a passion for the unprepossessing Grace Poole may support her suspicion that he now likes her. Recalling Rochester's impassioned looks and words of the night before, she trembles and blushes, which Adèle comments upon (the gist of the passage in French). So when she says that she 'hastened to drive' her hateful suspicion of Grace Poole from her mind, it is unclear whether she means the suspicion of attempted murder, or of Rochester's former passion for Grace Poole (which may now stand

for his present passion for Jane). She then compares herself mentally
with Grace Poole, reviewing Bessie's complimentary remarks on her
attractiveness. Charlotte Brontë has very cleverly retained Jane's
confusions in the narrative, and it seems likely that Jane's train of
thought is that as far as Rochester's sexual partner goes, she is better
fitted than Grace Poole, hence her blushing and confusion of ideas.
The idea that she is desired, and desires in return, peeps into her
consciousness before being quickly banished. The news of Blanche
Ingram, however, forces her to confront her desire without blench-
ing; but it has already been established that Jane is not a passive
female waiting to be chosen, but a woman with strong sexual desires
of her own, at the time a revolutionary and scandalous admission.

Chapter 17

Several weeks pass before Rochester returns with a numerous party
of visitors, including the Ingrams. Jane is required to make an
appearance in the drawing-room with Adèle, and sitting quietly in the
background she listens to the conversation. The talk eventually turns
to governesses, on which the Ingrams are particularly insulting.

Commentary
Jane's lack of personal attractiveness and class difference sorely try
her, and suffering from these insecurities Blanche Ingram's perfec-
tions seem all the more potent, a fear expressed in the language Jane
uses to describe her. For example, when Blanche first canters into
view Jane uses a heightened, romantic imagery: Blanche's purple
riding-habit sweeps the ground, while the wind tosses her veil and
raven ringlets. Jane broods on Blanche's advantages in order to
chasten her desires, but as Jane's experience in the drawing-room
attests, Blanche and her party are as morally coarse as they are
physically fine. The references to governesses are particularly informative. The party's indifference to Jane's presence underlines their
class arrogance, while the story of the dismissed lovers (the governess
and tutor) indicates a belief that hirelings lack even the basic right to
love. But Jane is not cowed by this society, and mentally cites the
Romantic belief in 'natural affinity' in stubborn defiance. As she
says, 'though rank and wealth sever us widely, I have something in
my brain and heart, in my blood and nerves, that assimilates me
mentally to him.' Blanche might be Rochester's equal physically and
socially, but not spiritually, and Jane rebelliously holds on to this
belief. Even so, Rochester's apparently indifferent behaviour is
clearly a trial to her.

Chapter 18

The party play charades, with one of the tableaux being a 'marriage' between Rochester and Blanche Ingram. Jane is uninvolved in these activities and her narrative becomes passive and introspective. She now believes Rochester intends to marry Miss Ingram, for family and 'political', not amorous, reasons. In her view the shallow and glittering Blanche cannot 'charm' Rochester, a failing which excites Jane's passion without feeding it hope. A day or so later, Rochester leaves the house on business, and a sallow visitor arrives, apparently fresh from the West Indies. The day's tedium is lifted by an old gypsy woman who now also appears, insisting on telling 'the quality' their fortunes. Miss Ingram goes first, returning in a foul temper. The other young women, having gone together, come back aglow with tales of the gypsy's clairvoyance. The chapter ends with a surprise summons for Jane, as the last unmarried woman – an invitation that gratifies Jane's burning curiosity.

Commentary
The chapter is strewn with clues which at this stage are difficult to make out. Blanche's angry disappointment may prelude the dashing of her matrimonial hopes, but other clues are less obvious. For example, what significance is there in the charade which ends with Rochester in chains? Note the detailed description of Mason (the sallow visitor), with his handsome but slack lineaments. Why is Jane so repelled by him, given the universal admiration his beauty excites? As we eventually learn, he is Mrs Rochester's brother. Does his character enlarge on hers? When you arrive at the description of Bertha Mason, it is worth comparing it with that of her brother.

Chapter 19

The gypsy's reading of Jane's heart and situation proves bizarrely acute, its uncanny directness wrapping Jane in a dreamy spell which Rochester snaps by breaking cover. Jane then relates Mason's arrival, a piece of news that disconcerts Rochester.

Commentary
The 'gypsy' prefers faces to palms as the more articulate book, thus bringing to a head the 'prenological' imagery. As Rochester says of Jane's mouth, 'it is disposed to impart all that the brain conceives', which partly suggests that Jane has a ready tongue, but more significantly it contrasts with Jane's earlier criticism of Blanche's

insincerity, her mouth not at all imparting what the brain conceives. Unlike Miss Ingram, Jane's face is an open book where the soul writes its character, a quality the mature Rochester clearly prefers to calculated dimples and smiles. In further reading her forehead he imparts a valuable insight into Jane's character, the firm control her reason has over her nevertheless turbulent passions. In his response Rochester avows his preference for spiritual nobility over perishing beauty, and his determination to bring her happiness. Although Jane can now have little doubt as to Rochester's feelings, she is still very guarded, and suppresses any mention of her elation.

Chapter 20

A piercing cry awakens the household. Mason has been knifed and bitten. Having calmed the others, Rochester asks Jane to tend Mason while he fetches the doctor, Mason being despatched from the house the moment he revives. Now dawn, Rochester invites Jane into the garden where he unburdens himself further, reverting once more to the theme of his reformation through a refreshing 'stranger'. At the crucial moment of declaration he hardens, tormenting Jane with references to Blanche.

Commentary
By conducting his love-making in disguise, Rochester seems bent on eliciting a declaration from Jane, with her throwing down her 'disguise' of caution, and openly avowing her love. Jane does not tell us what she is now feeling, so it is open to question whether she believes her love is requited, or whether she suppresses the hope. Whatever the case, this second crisis in the career of her passion once again coincides with an attack from Mrs Rochester.

In the latter half of this chapter Rochester nearly ceases to speak in riddles, however transparent, thus openly declaring himself. Such frankness occurs in the garden, an appropriate setting as the garden symbolises the freedom of nature. The house, on the other hand, is associated with wealth, rank and power, and so with social inhibitions and constraints. Even so, Rochester places Jane in an impossible position. He first tells her that he admires her precisely because she adheres so firmly to her conscience, and then encourages her to declare against custom, thus offending her conscience. Jane somewhat evasively replies that sinners should consult with God in their moment of crisis. Rochester presses her again, this time owning himself as the sinner, leaving his sentence open in the hope that she will complete it for him, thus confessing her love. To do so would be to capitulate, delivering herself to Rochester on his terms. She resists, and Rochester, piqued, retracts his expression of love, pretending that all along he really meant Blanche.

Chapter 21

Jane receives important tidings from Gateshead. Her cousin John has ended his dissipated life, inducing a fit of apoplexy in Mrs Reed, who now anxiously wishes to see Jane. Georgiana's and Eliza's characters are as they always were, only more pronounced, while Mrs Reed still loathes her niece. But, facing death, Mrs Reed desires to clear her conscience by confessing her last crime. Jane's uncle had written from Madeira requesting Jane's address in order to enrich her, but to spite her Mrs Reed replied that Jane was dead. The confession is timely, as Mrs Reed dies that very night.

Commentary
The chapter underlines the nature of Jane's transformations, her growth of character and morality, through a series of contrasts. Eliza and Georgiana are presented less as 'real' people, and more as 'humours' or types, the one inclining to feeling without judgement, the other to judgement without feeling. Jane, by comparison, is an even balance of both, which has the effect of rounding her out as a fictional character, and as a 'person'. The context of this contrast is Jane's overcoming of her childhood rage, which leads her to Christian forbearance and mature self-regulation. For a moment Mrs Reed's boorishness calls forth the old fire, but Jane triumphs over her vindictive feelings, and this enables her to forgive. Mrs Reed is set in stark contrast. Racked with guilt but unable to renounce her hatred, she repairs her injustices to Jane not out of generous, selfless feeling, but out of a selfish fear of death and its consequences. In this respect, the worst potential mischief Mrs Reed could have done to Jane was the subtle one of twisting her through hate, thus plunging her into the dehumanising selfishness that besets her children. The chapter underscores how triumphantly Jane has avoided this fate.

Thus we see that Jane has triumphed over her childish egotism, her burning desire for vengeance. Instead we find an equipoise of feeling and judgement, reflecting maturity and strength of character. How else is this generous but firm independence indicated in this chapter? If the novel charts Jane's growth of self – her coming to terms with her most powerful desires – is the journey now complete, and if not, what business is left unfinished? An additional, but not unconnected question you might consider is the purpose of the dream about the child at the beginning of the chapter. Is this Jane's superstition which we can discount, or is it hinting at something?

Chapter 22

Jane stays on at Gateshead for a month, attending first to Georgiana, and then to Eliza. Her return to Thornfield stirs up her ambivalent feelings. She is thrilled to return 'home' to Rochester, but depressed at his impending marriage to Blanche Ingram. Rochester intercepts her path, and is extremely genial. In the following weeks there is no sign of matrimonial preparation, and Jane's hopes revive.

Commentary
Jane tells us she is convinced of Rochester's marriage plans, but this melancholy belief is apparently contradicted by her irrepressible good spirits, and by the propitious weather as she approaches Thornfield (it 'promised well for the future'). The climatic imagery seems significant. The evening is warm, fiery and red, much as if the weather chimed her essential, passionate traits, so this must surely augur well. The signs are bright, she feels good, but her prospects are terrible. This disparity between feeling and expectation, meteorological splendour and amorous depression, serves several purposes. It heightens the tension as the reader's hopes revive with the weather, much as Jane's do. But it also suggests that Jane intuitively knows that Rochester will not marry Blanche, but that the knowledge is too potent to admit. She represses her hopes, from herself and reader alike.

Chapter 23

The summer continues hot and dry. Meeting in the garden at sunset, Rochester induces Jane to confess her feelings towards him, and then himself proposes. As they sit rapturously together, Rochester drops strange hints. In a moment of foreboding, the chestnut is struck by lightning.

Commentary
The pastoral imagery and the amorous 'sub-text' come to a climax here. The differing psychologies of Jane and Rochester derive from their social backgrounds and experience, gender and history. They do not speak their minds openly. On the contrary, their feelings and desires are subject to inhibitions, impulses to dominance and submission, evasiveness and fear. It is this lack of directness which creates the impression of character and psychology: if they spoke what they felt, if they had no interior lives, they would, as characters, appear flat and undeveloped. Nor would the drama have tension, the

suspense of indecision. This realm of the unspoken, which is hinted at and which the reader must piece together through inference, is what is meant by 'sub-text', the psychological jousting that takes place below the surface of the narrative, between the gaps of the revealed. Simply put, the characters play 'games', and it is up to the reader to deduce what the games are.

As noted earlier, the garden with its pastoral imagery is a site beyond the social, a scene of nature where the characters, 'outside' social constraints, are free to speak their inner feelings. Or rather, it is a place where the characters ought to be 'natural'. Moreover, the imagery of luxuriant vegetation and soft warming airs creates an erotic atmosphere, which blends human courtship with the innocent fecundity of nature. Rochester's cigar, and Jane's alertness, heightens the sexual tension. The episode of the moth suggests Jane's erotic vulnerability – a fatal attraction she cannot resist – while also suggesting that in the struggle of sexual politics, the balance is not equal. The hints of the imagery are thus played out 'sub-textually' in the conversation that follows.

Succumbing to the invitation of nature, Jane is predisposed to speak her mind. Rochester once more invites Jane to declare herself, only this time he keeps the upper hand by dwelling on Jane's fate rather than his own. He says Jane must leave, but promises to find her a situation in Ireland as a governess. Rochester's benevolent concern for Jane's welfare creates an intimacy between them, but this nearness is cruelly distanced by Rochester's references to her as a 'dependant'. Under the vulnerable circumstances this is too much for Jane, and she blurts out her love. Rochester continues to play his game of male and class dominance, where the final benediction of his reciprocated love is tantalisingly withheld until the final moment of gratifying condescension. But at the crucial moment Jane refuses the script, where she ought to play the meek and grateful dependant, or the helplessly attracted 'moth', and instead passionately declares her equality. Rochester endeavours to keep the game going by calling her a struggling 'bird', a role Jane contemptuously rejects. Indeed, so intense is Jane's passion that Rochester is forced to drop his mask, and declare his own. Nature has done its work, the two souls expressing their kindred in spite of the artificial barriers separating them. And yet all is not well. Rochester's predilection for playing games indicates his reluctance to accept Jane as an equal: repeatedly his turns of phrase cast her in a subservient role, with himself the condescending benefactor. This is inauspicious for the future, and the chapter ends with an omen signifying as much, the blasting of the chestnut under which the match has been sealed.

Chapter 24

The wedding is to be a month hence. The pattern of their engagement is set, with the lovers enthralled by one another. On hearing the news, Mrs Fairfax is sceptical of Rochester's motives. She conveys her suspicions to Jane.

Commentary
In many respects the interview with Mrs Fairfax strikes the keynotes of this chapter. Her dark hint that gentlemen are 'not accustomed to marry their governesses' reminds Jane of the social breach between them, and the precariousness of her situation. Mrs Fairfax also hints that Rochester's proposal is a seductive ruse. Accordingly the chapter ends with Jane adopting a teasing role that keeps Rochester on edge, and at a distance. More pertinently, Mrs Fairfax notes that Jane is a 'sort of pet of his', and much of the chapter is concerned with Rochester's domineering attitude, and Jane's rebellious response. Jane is likened to an angel, a fairy, and is even prized over the Grand Turk's entire seraglio; he wishes to dress her in finery, deck her in jewels; and finally, he wants to clip her to him, like his watch to his chain. Jane is once more put in a contradictory position. Rochester's 'despotism' demands 'lamb-like submission and turtle-dove sensibility', his judgement the reverse. As the paragraph immediately following the song indicates, there is an edge to Jane's plight. His 'falcon-eye' flashes, as if a ruthless, sexual bird of prey. For a moment Jane 'quails', which suggests that she is on the verge of becoming the passive object of his desire. Although she resists, evasion is not easy. As the concluding, retrospective paragraph points out, she had made an idol of Rochester, and she had rather capitulate than rebel.

Chapter 25

It is the day before the wedding and Jane is anxious and fretful. Rochester is away on business. Restless, Jane visits the garden. Meeting Rochester on his return, she tells him how on the evening before she dreamt again of the little child. In her dream she tries to catch up with the departing Rochester, but the child weighs her down. Jane slips and falls, which wakes her. At that moment she is disturbed by a strange woman in the room. Tall and dishevelled, and with a blotchy face, the woman rips Jane's wedding veil in two. Later Rochester tries to soothe Jane by blaming Grace Poole.

Commentary
The imagery of this section is particularly rich and suggestive (see
Section 5.1 below, and the examination of the specimen passage).
Jane fears there is a barrier between them, which there certainly is:
Mrs Rochester. But there are also barriers of other, more psycho-
logical kinds. These will be investigated in Section 5.2. Before turning
to it, interpret the chapter on your own, and then compare the
results.

Chapter 26

The day of the wedding begins with Rochester impatient, and Jane
anxious. Two mysterious strangers arrive, and at the crucial moment
they declare an impediment to the marriage. It is Mason and a
solicitor. Rochester confesses to having a wife, and then conducts the
party on a grisly inspection of the lunatic. The disaster leaves Jane
prostrate and depressed.

Commentary
Although Jane's confidence in Rochester is shattered, she blames
herself most: 'Oh, how blind had been my eyes! How weak my
conduct!' Superficially this is strange behaviour, for as Rochester
himself says, Jane has been blameless throughout. But we begin to
get an answer by attending to the mention of 'eyes'. As we saw at the
end of Chapter 24, Jane could not 'see God for his creature, of whom
[she] had made an idol'. Chapter 26 begins with Rochester calling
Jane 'the desire of his eyes', while Jane tells us that both her heart
and eyes had 'migrated into Rochester's frame'. It is traditional in
literary symbolism to equate eyes with erotic love, the mind with
spiritual love (for an example, see Shakespeare's *A Midsummer
Night's Dream*). To love with eyes rather than mind, or to let the eyes
guide the mind, is thus an unbalanced love that scants love's
immaterial aspects. Does this account for Jane's sense of guilt? In this
view the legal impediment to marriage would mirror an inner
unfitness, the amorous idolatry of letting erotic love outweigh other,
more sanctified kinds.

Chapter 27

Arising in the afternoon, Jane's conscience enjoins her to leave.
Rochester begs her to stay, proposing that they quit Thornfield for
the South of France. Jane refuses. To convince her of his honesty,
Rochester tells his story: the arranged marriage with Bertha Mason,

her gross infidelity, her eventual madness and, finally, his resolution to make a new life by leaving the West Indies for Europe, with Bertha incarcerated in Thornfield. But his narrative only hardens Jane's resolve by convincing her that she too must become one of Rochester's discarded mistresses. She flees as dawn breaks.

Commentary
The chapter marks a crisis in Jane's struggle between conscience and passion, duty and feeling. The phrase 'you shall yourself pluck out your right eye' once again echoes St Matthew, chapter five, in which she was drilled at Lowood, and as the Biblical source makes clear, the temptation is lust. This training now comes back to her in her moment of indecision to enforce her action. Although her passion is intense, conscience is stronger still, and she prepares to renounce the prospect of compromised pleasure. But conscience and reason turn traitor before Rochester's eloquent question: what is 'human law' compared with the certain despair of a 'fellow-creature'? Desire, reason and conscience thus combine, urging compliance with Rochester. Even so, she has reason enough left to realise her present 'insanity'. She takes refuge in her principles, her early religious training, and there she 'plants her foot', standing on the bedrock of Christian tenets. She is determined to leave, though it breaks both their hearts.

Charlotte Brontë always maintained that her books were not ethical tracts, but at this point the novel does seem to argue forcibly for traditional Christian morality. However, several ambiguities muddy the picture. First, the tenets that come to her aid were instilled at Lowood, so there may be a taint by association. Second, the closing, retrospective paragraph is far from certain in its conclusions. She hopes the reader may never, 'like me, dread to be the instrument of evil to what you wholly love.' This may mean that it is awful to do necessary harm to one you love; but there is also the suggestion that it is an avoidable, unnecessary dilemma. Finally, the moment when Jane's resolve is really cemented occurs in her room at night, when the moon shines on her in glorious brightness. As we shall see in Section 4.5, the moon figures as a kind of guardian spirit of Jane's (as well as an index of her emotions), hence its injunction to flee temptation, and her answer 'Mother, I will.' If the moon reflets Jane's inner development in a positive way, the suggestion arises that she acts not out of Christian duty, but out of 'duty' to herself – that it is essential to her development that she reject Rochester's terms. Does this self-preservation contradict the ethical motives, and hence the novel's Christian moralising?

Chapter 28

Two days later Jane finds herself bereft on the edge of the moors. She is soon reduced to fruitless beggary. Facing yet a third night in the open she nearly despairs, but a distant light rallies her spirits. She discovers a neat cottage, through the window of which she spies an elderly servant and two young gentlewomen. Their civilised looks convince her of a hospitable welcome, but the fearful servant refuses an interview. Jane's despairing appeal to God is overheard by an approaching young man, who ushers her in. Her intuition is proved right. She is given sustenance and a warm bed.

Commentary
The setting – the emptiness of the moors – underlines Jane's isolation. At the same time a contrast is drawn between nature – initially 'benign and good' – and the human community, which is mistrustful and rejecting. The orphan Jane does indeed seem an outcast, a misfit at odds with society, just as nature is. The description of the sisters thereby gains in significance, for they too are society's casualties, being 'graceful women', 'ladies in every point', yet in impoverished circumstances. Jane naturally identifies with them, and yearns to be part of their 'family'. At the same time the rustic simplicity of their surroundings, and their self-educating improvements, strongly hint that such an idyll is preferable to the luxurious refinements their 'class' would otherwise entitle them to.

Chapter 29

Jane is bedridden for three days, but rises on the fourth. She makes her peace with the servant, Hannah, who gives the history of the Rivers family. Jane then obliges St John with her story, suppressing all mention of the events at Thornfield. The minister promises to find Jane work.

Commentary
At this point the reader should become increasingly aware of a series of symmetries and oppositions. The Rivers siblings, like the Reeds, consist of two sisters and a brother, but the Rivers sisters are kind where the Reeds are not. And where John was large, stout and thick-featured, St John is slim and fair, with a Grecian profile. Where one was intemperate, the other is restrained; and whereas the Reeds squandered their privileges, the Rivers cultivate theirs, however slender in comparison. The Reeds rejected their relative, whereas the

Rivers adopt a stranger; a spirit of avarice runs through the one, Christian civility through the other. At the same time the Rivers are like Jane in being orphaned, and a further parallel is drawn between Jane and St John in that each detects in the other signs of forceful determination. A contrast is also drawn – albeit implicitly – between St John and Rochester, the former being as fair as the other is saturnine.

Chapter 30

Weeks pass quickly in the pleasurable company of the Rivers sisters, with whom Jane experiences a meeting of minds. Jane happily accepts St John's offer of becoming the parish school-mistress, but a pall settles over the rest of the family. St John is soon to leave on missionary work, the sisters as governesses. Necessity breaks the family circle, and the pastoral idyll at Moor House comes to a close. Tantalisingly, the Rivers learn that their rich uncle has just died, but left them nothing.

Commentary
The keynote of this chapter is the intrusion of the world of work: Diana and Mary must accept the demeaning employment of governess, compared to which Jane's school-teaching is a blessed relief as it doesn't involve a 'servitude with strangers'. For his part St John has his religious vocation. Accordingly, there is a thematic contrast between what the individual is suited to by 'nature' – the purpose of the idyll – and what society demands, with the consequent struggle of self-repression.

Chapter 31

Jane is reflecting on her first day's teaching when she is interrupted by St John who lectures her on the necessity of self-discipline, of curbing the bent of nature. The gorgeous Miss Oliver appears in the middle of his peroration to give ironic clarity to the terribleness of St John's own struggles.

Commentary
This is an exceedingly rich and tightly structured chapter. It begins in the present, with Jane in idealistic mood about the nobility of her job and subjects, but then switches to the past tense in which Jane, now looking back, admits to a then repressed feeling of degradation. This vacillation exemplifies her difficulties in reconciling passion and sense

of self to harsh duty. She then reviews her struggles with temptation in a puritanical way, concluding with a thankful prayer to providence for guiding her – but this may be a thinly veiled attempt to justify her present misery. St John then arrives on the scene, and correctly interpreting her tears as signs of regret, urges discipline and a higher reward upon her, but this advice is then almost immediately put in doubt by the perversity of his own self-abnegation. His ambition was worldly, but not his opportunities, so his speech smacks of justifying necessity. The arrival of Rosamund Oliver further undermines his position, for as Jane makes clear, the heiress is the perfection of nature, and glows with natural grace. Rosamund makes some trivial comments about the soldiers up to quell the 'riots'. St John sneers at Rosamund's superficiality, but this sexual teasing is very little different from Rochester's, which may excuse it in the reader's mind, but the puritanical St John chooses not to see it as harmless banter. Jane notes that the couple are perfect physical complements of each other – something St John's passion tells him only too well – and his strenuous rejection of Rosamund thereby seems a denial of nature's purpose. St John is clearly a parallel case to Jane, and the inadequacy of his self-justification for his repressive course casts worrying doubts over hers. You may wish to consider the contrary view that his course is perfectly justified.

Chapter 32

Jane increasingly enjoys her work, but is still dissatisfied. Rosamund Oliver visits her, and is so impressed with Jane's art that she requests a portrait. St John is startled by its likeness, and Jane uses the opportunity to probe his heart. The chapter ends with St John quitting the school in mysterious surprise.

Commentary
The parallel with St John now takes a twist. Jane is happy in work, but frustrated because unhappy in love. St John has the prospect of being happy in love, but rejects it for work. The chapter continues with its contrasting parallels, its repetition with difference. St John defends his refusal of Rosamund Oliver, on the grounds Rochester felt he should have adopted when considering marriage with Bertha Mason, namely that his passion is a 'fleshly fever' without a spiritual foundation. The difference occurs with Jane's scepticism. She is not unaware of Rosamund's moral and spiritual imperfections, so in arguing in favour of St John's union with her, she is implicitly repudiating the doctrine of self-sacrifice, of placing duty higher than

pleasure. In rejecting Rochester, Jane subordinated passion to conscience; but now she believes that conscience should defer to passion, in St John's case at least, but this may also indicate that she is undergoing a change of mind. What comparisons can you make between St John and Rochester, and what do they signify?

Chapter 33

St John bursts in upon Jane on a snowy winter's day anxious to confirm his suspicions, which prove just. Jane Elliott is indeed Jane Eyre, the heiress of their uncle in Madeira, and cousin to the Rivers. Jane immediately decides on splitting the money with her relatives, with the purpose of uniting her 'new found' family.

Commentary
Whereas Jane is passionate and impetuous, St John is cool and detached, and Charlotte Brontë turns this to account in heightening the dramatic tension. St John burns with a mystery, but coolly delays investigation, thus tantalising the reader. Instead of asking Jane her identity point blank, he spins a story – Jane's, as it turns out. The detail of Rochester catches us up before St John brings us round to the main point: Mr Eyre's death and Jane's inheritance. But St John leaves a gap – how he came by this information – and is prepared to leave without filling it in; even when pressed, he only hints. As a consequence we share Jane's dawning realisation, and rejoice with her, not in the accession of fortune, but in the acquisition of a family; as the pieces fall into place for her, they do for us, and so that we vicariously experience that most potent of romances, the gaining of family, once lost and now found.

Chapter 34

The chapter begins with a scene of domestic bliss. It is Christmas and, together with Hannah, Jane sets about preparing for the sisters' happy return. They clean the house from top to bottom, set fires blazing, and make copious quantities of cakes. But St John is cold and miserably reserved. He requests that Jane assist him in learning Hindustani, and once spring arrives, he declares his plan: Jane must join him as a missionary in India. After some agonising Jane gives her assent, as long as they do not marry. St John insists, and the chapter ends in stalemate.

Commentary

When Jane refused Rochester, she did so because of Christian principle; St John now invites Jane to serve that principle in its extreme form, as a self-sacrificing missionary. Jane realises it will mean the literal death of her, and the figurative death of one half of her character. Despairing of finding Rochester, she is prepared to accept the first, but not the second. Marriage to St John would not only be a 'counterfeit', but, as his speech makes clear, he wants her as an instrument in God's work, but at St John's total command. She is prepared to accept the domination of her ethical, but not her deeper, desiring self. This the marriage would compromise, and here she rebels, to St John's infinite chagrin.

Chapter 35

Jane attempts to propitiate St John, but only offends him further. Diana questions Jane, and when she discovers St John's plan, urges the folly of acceptance. But that night St John reads from Revelations, and in the religious ecstasy of the moment, and under St John's now gentle urging, Jane nearly submits. In her moment of vacillation, she entreats heaven for a sign. Mysteriously, she hears Rochester's voice.

Commentary

The complementary nature of Jane's two 'marriage' proposals – with their crises of indecision – is fully revealed in this chapter, something Jane herself draws attention to. To have accepted the one would have been an error of 'principle', the other an error of 'judgement'. Both proposals are shams, the one legally so, the other emotionally. Rochester's would mean sacrificing principle to pleasure. St John's the reverse. Under the spell of veneration for St John, Jane is tempted to cease struggling, 'to rush down the torrent of his will into the gulf of his existence, and there lose my own'. So in both crises of indecision she feels tempted to abandon herself to domineering male wills, and in both – almost as a matter of instinctive self-preservation – she refuses, rebelliously sticking out for her independence.

Chapter 36

Convinced of the significance of her aural 'hallucination', Jane is determined to seek Rochester at Thornfield. Once there, fearing to ask news, she coyly approaches, only to discover Thornfield a blackened ruin. The innkeeper relates the story, first telling us what we already know, and then what we do not. We learn of Rochester's depression on Jane's leaving, and then of Bertha Mason escaping the notice of a drunk Grace Poole, to set fire to the house. Rochester flies to her rescue, but as he approaches she jumps to her death. Tragically, a beam falls on him as he negotiates the burning wreck, leaving him a blind cripple.

Commentary
Although Jane is convinced Rochester needs him, she still sees his wife as an insurmountable impediment. The news of her death immediately changes that. Note once again Charlotte Brontë's dramatic technique of delaying information, first through Jane's indecisive dallying as she approaches, and second by having the doddering butler tell the story. It is conventional for the old to be garrulous, and Charlotte Brontë uses this to heighten the tension.

Chapter 37

Having heard the innkeeper's tale, Jane immediately orders a chaise, and hurries to Ferndean. Chapter 37 begins with her arrival. Jane reveals herself to the blind Rochester, and in the course of that night and the next day, Rochester courts her anew. Jane accepts his proposal, and the chapter ends with Rochester's revelation of his appeal, which perfectly coincides with Jane's hearing of the voice, in time, place and reply. She is awed by this, and not wishing to disturb Rochester, conceals her experience.

Commentary
Jane believes that Rochester will immediately claim her, and initially interprets his diffidence as a reluctance to do so. She soon realises that he fears rejection in his battered state, but does not enlighten him. Indeed, she teases him with jealousy, forcing Rochester to frame his proposal anew. This prolongs the emotional scene, but at the same time it serves to underline Jane's independent strength. He must come to her, not the reverse (itself a contrast with the first proposal); and thematically this links with her new found position of equality. As she says, 'I love you better now, when I can really be useful to you, than I did in your state of proud independence, when you disdained every part but that of the giver and protector.' Can one go further and say that Jane has now adopted the dominant role, and Rochester the submissive?

Chapter 38

Jane touches upon the present in drawing together her story's remaining threads, a point ten years after her marriage to Rochester. We learn how fruitful and happy this union has been, how Adèle was properly educated, and how Mary and Diana married happily. The final words are devoted to St John, in praise of his sacrifice, and the certainty of his reward, now rapidly approaching.

Commentary
It is the nature of love romances to end with marriage, so in this respect *Jane Eyre* is true to type. The servants are pleased, others marry, children arrive, the relationship between Rochester and Jane is equal and loving, and Rochester partially regains his sight. But a number of questions do suggest themselves. Why does Jane reserve her last words for St John? Is there any difficulty in reconciling the earlier, independent Jane with the picture we now have of the contented housewife? And is the ending suspiciously idyllic, too much like a fairy tale come true? Such questions suggest that the harmony is not as complete as it seems. You may wish to take the contrary view that the harmony is just as Jane tells us, and that the ending represents the triumph of love over personal difficulty and social difference.

3 THEMES AND ISSUES

3.1 GROWING UP

As we have seen, the novel tells us the story of Jane's 'growing up'. The critical term for novels of this type is *Bildungsroman*, or 'novel of education'. In reviewing her history Jane tells us about central events in the development of her character. The novel's many themes and issues arise out of this process of learning.

In growing up Jane experiences many crises which force her into crucial judgements and decisions. Not all her decisions are conscious ones. For example, her response to John Reed's tormentings is a spontaneous rebellion. In that sense her 'insurrection' is not a decision at all, but a trusting to instinct. Even so, her rebellion is a crucial phase in her growing up, one having a profound influence on her subsequent career. Her decisions to leave Rochester, and then to return, are also 'intuitive' or instinctive in so far as both depend on mysterious interventions (the dream 'mother' in the one case, Rochester's voice in the other). Elsewhere, however, Jane is very deliberate in what she does, such as when she determines on finding a new servitude, or when she tries to live up to Helen Burns's Christian teachings.

This balance between conscious and unconscious decision-making is central to the process by which *Jane Eyre* presents its themes. 'Unconscious' decision-making can be roughly identified with 'instinct', and hence with 'nature'. Conscious decisions, insofar as they conform with society's values and morals, can be identified with 'nurture'. Nature versus nurture: this basic opposition creates a dominating thematic tension in *Jane Eyre*. *Jane Eyre* is rich in themes, but they tend to be variations on this central one.

The point can be made if we look more closely at the book's structure. There are five central episodes: Jane's childhood in the

Reed household at Gateshead; her school days at Lowood; her time as a governess at Thornfield; the period as a school teacher at Morton; and her spell at Ferndean which ends with her marriage to Rochester. Each episode is identifiable with a crucial stage in Jane's development. At Gateshead Jane is exposed to a 'conventional' family environment where she is expected to conform; Lowood presents her with contrasting varieties of religious experience (those of Brocklehurst and Helen Burns); Thornfield introduces love; Morton emphasises work and duty. The events at Ferndean leading to the marriage are the final 'stage', the culmination of Jane's development, and in this respect the marriage represents the resolution of earlier themes. With marriage, the conflicts come to an end.

In relating the history of her inner self, her 'growing up', Jane organises her 'life' into core episodes, each one touching upon a central human experience: family life, education, love, work, and then marriage. Each of these core episodes provides Jane with choices peculiar to the central experiences they involve. So although in each instance Jane may have to decide between following her instinct or her reason, her feeling or judgement, desire or conscience (and thus broadly between what she knows by nature, and what by nurture) the circumstances, and therefore the thematic shading, is different in each case. The 'theme' may be the same, but each episode introduces significant variations.

In the following sections we will be looking at this central theme from varying angles. But before we do so it may help to look at the core opposition more closely.

It is here raised by St John Rivers. St John has just confessed to Jane that 'Reason, and not feeling, is my guide: my ambition is unlimited; my desire to rise higher, to do more than others, insatiable' (Chapter 32). Jane reasonably rejoins that St John is a 'pagan philosopher', as he seems devoted to worldly fame, and not God. St John defends himself by saying that his ambition does indeed serve religion:

Won in youth to religion, she has cultivated my original qualities thus: From the minute germ, natural affection, she has developed the overshadowing tree, philanthropy. From the wild stringy root of human uprightness she has reared a due sense of the divine justice . . . So much has religion done for me; turning the original materials to the best account; pruning and training nature. But she could not eradicate nature; nor will it be eradicated 'till this mortal shall be put on immortality' (Chapter 32).

Notice St John's choice of metaphors. Benevolent feelings for others ('natural affection') is a 'minute germ', a seed easily crushed or destroyed. 'Human uprightness' is a 'stringy', unpromising root. St John is using an extended metaphor to get his ideas across, and in this instance he draws it from horticulture, the art of gardening. The metaphor draws out the theme of nature versus nurture, and it ends with 'eradicated', which means to 'pluck up by the roots'. St John clearly holds pessimistic views regarding his 'original materials', which he believes to be untrustworthy, at best. In his view 'nurture', or education, is clearly desirable. If reason cannot 'eradicate' feeling, it should at least subdue it.

The implication of St John's point of view is that childhood is bad, for then we are most natural, and least touched by nurture. This helps raise the thematic idea that in growing up, and in coming into conflict with others, Jane should submit to 'teaching', relinquishing her natural desires. St John's thinking has a long history in Western culture, but another, contrary point of view had recently become popular as a result of the Romantic movement which had swept Europe some fifty years before the publication of *Jane Eyre*.

The Romantic poet most closely associated with this point of view is William Wordsworth (1770–1850). In poems such as *The Prelude* and the 'Immortality' ode, he argued that growing up was not the gaining of wisdom, but the losing of it; or, as he memorably puts it, in growing up 'Shades of the prison-house begin to close' upon the child. Weaning a child from nature and his natural proclivities, far from wise, was a tragic hastening of a descent into mediocrity, the soul burdened with an 'earthly freight'. 'Custom', rather than a reservoir of wisdom, comes to sit upon the child as a deep 'frost'. One gained the instinct of religion – a sense of the quickening spirit of God that ennobles human life – not through religious nurture, as St John believes, but from nature itself, in which this spirit exists as a haunting 'presence'. In Wordsworth's view, the child had an innate feeling and understanding for the quick of nature. Hence Wordsworth's famous phrase, 'the child is father to the man', meaning that it is the child who lays up rich store for the adult by his instinctive openness to nature. In this respect the child 'fathers' his later self through his early education, the one that truly matters, and from which his adult self derives. Wordsworth effectively reverses St John's view by placing the higher value on nature.

St John values nurture and distrusts nature; Wordsworth does the reverse. As we shall see, *Jane Eyre* contains both outlooks. To the degree that the novel favours 'nature', spontaneous responses of the self are valued, such as instinct, feeling, desire; but if nurture, then reason, judgement, constraint. Where the weighting falls is finally a matter of interpretation. There is also the possibility that the novel refuses to draw a simple either/or.

3.2 SELF AND SOCIETY

In the previous section we noted that in the process of growing up Jane makes many decisions, some 'instinctive', others conscious. In one respect her decisions represent Jane trying to find a balance between childish passion and adult judgement – a 'balance' because either extreme could be damaging. For instance, a child who never 'tamed' her passions would be unbearable and egotistic, much like the older Georgiana, who arguably does not grow up. On the other hand, to be entirely 'reasonable', as Mrs Reed defines it, holds the threat of self-denial and self-effacement. Hence the irony in Mrs Reed saying that Jane shall be 'liberated' from the red-room 'only on condition of perfect submission' (Chapter 2). Clearly, there is not much point to 'liberation' if it depends upon submissive docility. Such excessive obedience is a threat to selfhood. But the corresponding danger of too little is that the child would never lose its egotistic propensities. Growing up partially consists of finding a proper balance between these extremes.

As we see, to talk about instinct and judgement quickly involves us in talk about freedom and constraint. The individual may wish to do as he or she pleases, but society requires conformity. Each individual must come to terms with society, must curb the self's desires, but the problems and difficulties will vary depending on one's station in life. Jane Eyre's perspective is conditioned by her sex and class, by the trials attending a poor but educated middle-class woman's attempts at finding a happy balance between what she wants and what society requires.

The opposition between Romanticism and rationality provides one perspective on this struggle. The Romantic view would be that one may justifiably rebel against social conformity. Jane feels a constant pressure rationally to conform with society's demands, to accept the limiting facts of her class and sex. But Jane pushes against these limits, fighting convention in order to keep a space clear for her inner life. When Charlotte Brontë gives us panoramic glimpses into Jane's imaginative world, she appears to support Jane's rebellion. Jane's dreams, reveries, pictures and speech reveal an inner richness which ought not to be stifled, but expressed.

The great attraction of the book, however, is that it goes beyond the somewhat abstract opposition of Romanticism and rationality, giving us a wealth of concrete instance. Jane's background and conditioning are sharply realised, as is the milieu in which she moves. As a result, her choices are both particular and socially typical. The two great facts of her existence are precisely examined. As a woman, she has only one real avenue for self-expression: marriage. For the male Romantic poets, the struggle between self and society tended to resolve into the opposition between the spiritually suffocating city, with its restricted ways of thinking and feeling, and the world elsewhere that was nature, a contrasting place of spiritual freedom. For Jane, the matter is not so simple. She cannot simply retire to a place in the country. Economic necessity dictates work, but the work available turns on self-sacrifice. To be a governess, as the drawing room scene amply demonstrates, is to fall into a state of non-being, a no-man's land between the domestics and the quality. A governess lives for the education and training of her charges, but her class position is such that she has no means of disciplining them. The class structure rules out free expression with those above and below her, and this leaves her isolated. Employed to set an example, her position immediately rules out any love interest she might have with her class equal, the children's tutor, should such a being luckily exist. Even the subjects she teaches are narrow, being largely music, sewing, painting, foreign languages (if fortunate), a restricted realm of intellectual activity that compromised her other alternative, that of school-teaching. Being a school-teacher did have one advantage, greater freedom, but this was lost in the very severe conditions of service. Charlotte Brontë repeatedly refuses to give glamour to these occupations by throwing over them a glowing mantle of noble self-sacrifice. Jane gains credit in St John's eyes through her devotion to her charges as the village school-teacher, and to an extent Jane draws satisfaction at making progress. But she immediately drops it once her financial freedom is secured. There is no misplaced idealism here. Jane refuses to be a martyr.

Jane's employment prospects hold few opportunities for self-cultivation, and the alternative is scarcely better. Marriage might lift a woman out of grinding economic dependence, but it threw her into yet another servitude. Here, too, Jane rebels against conformity, although her reaction is not outright revolt. Rather she is made uneasy by dominant male wills, and while at times she feels inclined to yield, at others her resolve stiffens. This is especially so when her equality is threatened, usually causing her to dig in her heels. Interestingly, the plot eventually sees to the establishment of this equality. Rochester's physical disabilities (and Jane's sudden acquisition of wealth) put them on a more equal footing, while serving at a symbolic level to enforce the desirability of such equality. It is even arguable that Jane assumes a superior position.

The struggle between self and society is thus represented in Jane's resisting society's institutions regarding work and marriage. But she is not the only casualty, real or potential. Rochester himself is alienated from society, a victim of the rule of primogeniture which forces him into a marriage of convenience; nor will society's rigid divorce laws allow dissolution. But a more salient figure is St John Rivers, to an extent Jane's male equivalent. Like her he is a member of the upper middle class fallen on hard times. He is in possession of superior talents, and like her he is passionate and ambitious. As he tells Jane, he

> burned for the more active life of the world – for the more exciting toils of a literary career – for the destiny of an artist, author, orator, anything rather than that of a priest: yes, the heart of a politician, of a soldier, of a votary of glory, a lover of renown, a luster after power, beat under my curate's surplice. (Chapter 31).

The church was as inevitable a choice of career for St John as governess was for Jane, and as frustrating. But then a light fell, bringing relief, and reconciliation with his lot: he would go to India as a missionary. In the light of the novel's thematic interest in the competing claims of self and society, St John's motives seem highly questionable. He means to imply that missionary work is desirable because of its intrinsic merits, but then he says 'the best qualifications of soldier, statement, and orator, were all needed', which suggests that he is reconciled to the Church on the grounds that it affords an outlet for worldly ambition after all.

So, like Jane, St John is deeply frustrated by society's inability to meet his needs for a challenging and stimulating vocation, but unlike her he makes a virtue of necessity, finding positive qualities in his servitude. Interestingly, his arguments in favour of justification through good works – which he alludes to, to bolster his choice – bear a close resemblance to Brocklehurst's arguments; and just as we saw Brocklehurst use religious language as a means of implementing social control, so it may appear that St John is a victim of that control, a casualty of its self-denying rhetoric. As we shall see in the next section, there is additional evidence to support this inference, that St John's choice is an unnatural perversion of his legitimate passion for self-fulfilment. Whereas Jane listens to the voice of her innermost feelings, St John self-denyingly shuts his out. What is important here, however, is the final complexity of the novel's observation of the struggle between self and society. Society does not merely cramp the individual by the limited life-choices it offers the less fortunate; it also does so through its language of values, which invites the individual to embrace his servitude as a morally good thing, which it may indeed be. But the novel also allows us to see St John's choice as a self-destructive martyrdom, as a good choice for society, but a bad one for St John. If one believes that St John is a casualty of society's self-denying rhetoric, then one may also entertain suspicions regarding Jane's insistence that she was right to deny herself Rochester when he proposed they should go to France.

3.3 NATURE VERSUS GRACE

Jane Eyre makes repeated reference to 'nature' and 'grace', and many of its thematic concerns are tied up with the religious nuances of these words. Helen Burns, Brocklehurst and St John Rivers represent three different religious attitudes, and while none of them is strictly speaking a Methodist, the issues their religious views highlight are inextricably tied to the rise of Methodism, which occurred in the eighteenth century as part of the Evangelical revival.

Evangelicism is distinguished by two central tenets, the primacy of the Bible as the origin of divine revelation, and justification by faith. This meant that the experience of religious conversion, of being possessed by Christ, was itself sufficient to guarantee salvation. Evangelists urged their audiences to open their hearts to God; if one did, and one was gripped with religious enthusiasm, then one was saved. In such circumstances one was in a state of 'grace'.

The Evangelical preacher John Wesley (1703–91) was the founder of Methodism, and at the end of the eighteenth century his movement split in a number of crucial ways. The first split concerned the movement's relationship with the established Church. Although Wesleyan Methodism was highly conservative, it was viewed suspiciously by the established Church, who would not allow Wesley to ordain his own priests. As a consequence this strand of the Evangelical movement split between those who remained within the Church of England, and those 'Methodists' who kept faith with the new church.

A second important division occurred within the ranks of this new church (Methodism proper), and here the precipitating cause was a dispute over the issue of justification through faith. Wesley had maintained that salvation was open to all, but a Calvinist element in the movement argued that salvation was available only to the 'elect', to those predestined for heaven. A belief in predestination is the distinguishing feature of Calvinism. God knew who was predestined for heaven and who wasn't, so one could not force His hand through 'good works'; if you were not one of the chosen, no amount of do-gooding would help. The Wesleyan Methodists believed both in justification by faith and justification through good works, whereas the hard-line Calvinist Methodists disputed both.

As the nineteenth century progressed, Wesleyan Methodism predominated, while also becoming increasingly conservative in outlook; as it did so, justification through good works took gradual precedence over justification through faith. Clearly, those in possession of wealth had greater scope for good works than the poor, and here an important modification of Methodism, and Evangelicism, takes place. Although Wesleyan Methodists, and Evangelicals within the bosom of the established Church, could distance themselves from Calvinism on specific points of Christian theology, there was a far greater interpenetration of attitudes common to both, which is understandable if one remembers that these movements all derived from the same Protestant creeds. It was a Calvinist habit to probe one's conscience for signs of one's 'election' (meaning that one was destined for heaven); if it were a mass of illicit desires, there was not much hope. But there were other signs as well, such as personal prosperity. If God foreknew who was saved and who wasn't, it followed that God would only visit material prosperity on those who were cut out to do His work in order to accomplish it better. Hard-line Calvinists disputed this, but even so, the 'corrupt' Calvinist attitude that wealth signified election took hold, becoming a pervasive Victorian prejudice. As everything was foreknown, it followed that prosperity had God's blessing, and was indeed a sign of His approval, part of His providential design. Wealth thus became an infallible marker of grace, and poverty an equally unmistakable sign of its absence. This hardened into the familiar Victorian prejudice (frequently attacked by Dickens) that the poor deserved their poverty. Its equally familiar corollary was that, if wealth betokened grace, so poverty signified immorality.

In the highly polarised Victorian society these were clearly issues of great moment. The aspirations of the poor were particularly troublesome as they questioned the basis of social power. Institutionalised Evangelicism with its 'corrupt' Calvinist strain (whether within the established Church or Methodism proper) offered a means of regularising these aspirations, providing a benediction for success while stigmatising failure. A poor man who successfully pulled himself up by his bootstraps could be admitted to the ranks of the middle class, as his prosperity signified his inner spiritual worth. Failure, on the other hand, could be fairly laid at the door of the individual, and not society. Brocklehurst perfectly exemplifies this way of thinking. The rich need not worry about their spiritual condition as their wealth guaranteed their possession of grace; but the poor, being poor, clearly had to watch out for theirs – hence his admonitions to the poor girls to scrutinise the state of their souls. This attitude had a convenient consequence. Given the unspoken premise regarding the sinfulness of the poor, it followed that their energies should be turned to other objects than material prosperity, and certainly not to pleasure, as these temptations would surely deepen their sinfulness. It justified the status quo while scotching the validity of ambition. The girls of Lowood should not have worldly ambitions, but should starve their vile bodies while feeding their immoral souls, in their case nourished through self-denial.

One way of typifying Brocklehurst's hypocrisy was that there was to be Evangelicism for the rich, and Calvinism for the poor. Where the rich could recline in the Evangelical confidence of being in a state of grace, justified as they were by such good works as Lowood, the poor could not. As an Evangelical, Brocklehurst might reasonably believe that his charges could at least take recourse in justification through faith, but this is apparently not the case. The girls are not simply encouraged to open their hearts to God, they are urged to experience the high anxiety of Calvinist introspection, of permanently scanning their consciences for signs of grace or, darkly, for signs of its absence (and therefore of eternal damnation).

In this respect Helen Burns offers an eloquent, if implicit, rebuke to Brocklehurst. At the beginning of Chapter 8, Helen offers solace to Jane by saying that Jane's inner conviction of innocence should be enough, and elsewhere she advocates her 'democratic' doctrine of the 'equality of disembodied souls', that is to say, she advocates the more generous Evangelical tenets of justification by faith, and salvation for all, from which Brocklehurst's brand of Evangelicism has deviated. Helen's is the ideal by which we measure the corrupt distance Brocklehurst has travelled. That Helen should be persecuted is the final, ironic turn of the screw.

Another rebuke is offered by St John Rivers, who is Brocklehurst's opposite in some important respects. Whereas Brocklehurst is a religious hypocrite, St John is sincere; and whereas the former has his class interest at heart in the school he superintends, St John has his pupils' interests. If Brocklehurst is a model of what Evangelical ministers too often are, St John is a model of what they should be; or at least one might think so given the book's parting respect for St John's approaching martyrdom (Chapter 38). But there is a harsh Calvinist element in St John's Evangelicism, as when he doubts Jane is really one of 'the chosen' when she rejects his plan (Chapter 35). If Brocklehurst fails the Helen Burns test, so does St John.

We are now in a position to appreciate how biting the religious irony is in *Jane Eyre*. As stated earlier, Helen Burns, Brocklehurst and St John Rivers are not strict Methodists, but they are Evangelicals, and their attitudes towards grace are telling. In fact it is possible to see in these three figures representations of the main divisions in Methodism, with Helen Burns representing the early 'democratic' impulse of the Evangelical movement, Brocklehurst its corrupt entanglement with social power, and the Calvinistical St John its harsh, 'purist' strain. We should not see these figures as possible options for Jane to follow; rather they mark out the field for Jane's struggles.

Thus we see that 'nature' and 'grace' involved crucial social issues as the conformity they urged supported the political status quo. *Jane Eyre* questions the conformist meanings of these terms in several ways.

The first occurs at the level of plot. More conventional domestic romances enforced Brocklehurst's viewpoint by denying its humbler heroines happiness in this life if they did not lower their matrimonial sights. *Jane Eyre* marks a decisive break with this pattern with Jane marrying Rochester and living happily ever after. This is one in the eye for Brocklehurst, with his grim warnings that girls of Jane's sort had only self-mortification to look forward to in this life. It also implies that spiritual worth cuts across class boundaries, and that Jane is every bit as 'good' as Rochester.

A second way in which the novel argues against the conformist meanings of 'nature' and 'grace' is more complex, and relates back to our earlier discussion of the transformation of attitudes that distinguished Romanticism. Traditionally 'nature' and 'grace' had fairly stable meanings. In the modern world nature was fallen, and one had to work hard to achieve grace. But as we have seen, Romanticism tended to question this view, frequently seeing nature as innocent, as being itself 'graceful'. In this respect the terms 'nature' and 'grace' became contentious, and their meanings less clear-cut. *Jane Eyre* shares this semantic scepticism. For example, there is a scathing irony when Brocklehurst says to Mrs Reed that he trusts Jane will 'show herself grateful for the inestimable privilege of her election [to Lowood]'. 'Election' is a Calvinist word; when one was in a state of grace, one joined the 'elect' who were destined for heaven. Brocklehurst identifies joining Lowood with joining heaven – a grotesque equation, as we eventually see. And nature, far from being the state of unregenerative savagery from which the children must be saved, is pictured as a pastoral innocence from which the children have been cruelly removed. This inversion of nature and grace recurs throughout the book, and most importantly in the love scenes between Jane and Rochester that occur in gardens, where the weather tends to be good. One cannot say with perfect justification that Rochester and Jane are a modern Adam and Eve, but the pastoral beauty of their surroundings does suggest a similar innocence and rightness. When Jane begins to chasten herself for loving across the divide of rank and wealth, she reproves her misgivings as 'Blasphemy against nature!' (Chapter 17). So rather than sinful longings in need of repression, her desires are portrayed as innocent, natural, and bestowed with grace.

The same point is emphatically made near the end of the novel. St John's vision of a life of duty and grace fills Jane with veneration. She nearly yields, but Rochester's voice interrupts, and Jane pointedly believes it to be the 'work of nature' (Chapter 35). St John offers grace, but Jane hearkens to nature. Moreover, the collective force of the imagery is to support nature as an innocent good, and this is enough to throw doubt on the reliability of St John's version of grace.

The doubt creeps in at many levels. For example, Chapter 30 begins with a glowing description of nature, with its 'sweet and pure sources of pleasure'. Diana and Mary share Jane's enthusiasm for the scenery, but the restless St John is indifferent to it. In Romantic writing openness to the beauties of nature was a standard test of a character's spiritual mettle. St John's indifference leaves a question mark hanging over his.

Charlotte Brontë's cunning inversion of the conventional romance plot also implants doubt. In the usual 'happy' *dénouement* the heroine accepts a class equal as her husband, or a self-sacrificing social role. This is precisely what St John offers, so at this point the novel seems destined for conventionality, but then resumes its radical career. Charlotte Brontë's repudiation of this plot matches Jane's repudiation of martyrdom, which leaves St John the mouthpiece of destructive blandishments. If Jane's story is a succession of trials that test her strength, then St John's honeyed speech on the glories of self-sacrifice is the final snare. As Jane says, to have accepted would have been 'an error of judgement' (Chapter 35).

A final reason for pessimism emerges if we look at the novel structurally. St John's spurning of Rosamund parallels Jane's refusal of Rochester, as both place principle above passion. Jane now has

time to reflect. Not only does she urge St John to marry Rosamund – such as she still wishes to marry Rochester, if she were
able – but the language used to describe Rosamund is highly significant. She is nature's 'darling', and moves with 'native grace' (Chapter
31). In Jane's eyes, at least, the salvation St John searches for is
standing in front of him. St John's refusal of Rosamund mirrors
Jane's earlier situation, and while Jane's reason might defend her
original decision, her approving language (of Rosamund) suggests
emotional regret. In this context St John's behaviour feels particularly perverse. Finally, St John's views on grace are an uncomfortable
echo of Brocklehurst's.

In conclusion, we see that 'nature' and 'grace' were important
terms for Charlotte Brontë, as they raised crucial thematic issues. As
we have seen, Brocklehurst believes that girls in Jane's position
should pursue 'grace' and repress 'nature'. He believes grace to be
good, and nature bad. At the end Jane may believe the opposite, but
to an extent that is not the point. Fundamental questions regarding
the self's inherent goodness or badness have been raised in a realistic
and yet complex way, and it is up to engaged readers to decide the
issue for themselves.

3.4 PASSION VERSUS REPRESSION

'Freedom' and 'constraint' are other terms which may help us think
about the opposition between passion and repression. By 'freedom'
one means the unhampered expression of desire; by 'constraint', the
doing of what society wants, rather than what 'you' want. In Section
3.2 we looked at this as a conflict between the individual and social
institutions, such as work and marriage. This section examines the
more general forces that would encourage 'constraint', and the
novel's attitude towards them. The thematic points of interest occur
as confrontations between desire and 'repressive' forces, and fall into
three overlapping areas of experience: the social, the religious, and
that of 'sexual politics'.

Social repression begins at Gateshead. What is appropriate for the
Reed sisters is inappropriate for the dependant. Where the former
are 'dressed out in thin muslin frocks and scarlet sashes, with hair
elaborately ringleted', Jane is not (Chapter 4). Indeed, throughout
the book the upper-class women are seen in dress that accentuates
their attractions, for example Georgiana, the Brocklehurst girls,
Blanche Ingram and Rosamund Oliver. By contrast, Jane is restricted
to the sexually modest. This is made expressly clear in Chapter 5,

where Jane finds it an 'oddity' to see the grown girls at Lowood dressed with such severe plainness, with high 'brown dresses . . . woollen stockings and country-made shoes'. The scene typifies general differences. Whereas Georgiana and her ilk are encouraged to have marital expectations, Jane and her ilk are not. The unspoken message behind these contrasts is that girls in Jane's position should suppress their desires, given their likely careers as productive spinsters.

The double standard we see emerging at Gateshead, with Jane treated one way, her cousins another, is given religious support at Lowood. Where the Brocklehurst girls arrive with their bouncing curls, the inmates of Lowood have theirs combed out. The 'philosophy' behind this regime is revealed in a scene both comic and serious. Brocklehurst reprimands Miss Temple for Julia Severn's curls. Miss Temple patiently points out that Julia's hair curls naturally, thus provoking Brocklehurst's wrath: 'Naturally! Yes, but we are not to conform to nature. I wish these children to be the children of Grace' (Chapter 7). Equating naturally curling hair with vicious propensities is clearly absurd, but for the girls the joke has a sour taste, for if they are to be 'children of Grace', they must repress their passions (the context makes it clear that this is the 'nature' Brocklehurst means). This prepares us for the inversion of 'grace' and 'nature' analysed in the previous section. The important point here, however, is to note the way the Lowood scenes represent the repressive climate in which Jane moves, with Calvinist terror and Methodistical morality jointly mobilising against passion in Jane and the other girls.

Repressive forces are also to be found in the realm of sexual politics, and here too Jane rebels. For example, Rochester habitually praises Jane for her doll-like qualities; in effect, he speaks of her as an object. Jane cunningly recognises that if she accepts the role Rochester imagines for her, that of toy, he will likely soon tire, much as a spoilt child would. As she puts it, 'a lamb-like submission and turtle-dove sensibility' would have 'fostered his despotism more', and pleased his judgement, common sense and taste less (Chapter 24). Instead, she keeps him on edge through her 'system' of teasing replies. As this is a deep source of her attraction to him, the strategy has a practical merit. Even so, it is a hazardous course in which the full perversity of the male mind is revealed, where Jane must resist Rochester's advances in order to keep the both of them happy. But beneath the comic surface of this sparring a very real danger lurks, in some ways worse than seduction and abandonment, and that is that Jane's independent being should lose itself in Rochester's imperious will. And just as there is a repressive threat in Rochester's vigorous courtship – the threat of becoming Rochester's toy – so there is in St John's appeal to duty. To please him, she finds, is to 'disown half my nature'; joining St John in India is to 'abandon half myself' (Chapter 34); and finally, in his visionary appeal to religious self-sacrifice, she finds herself tempted to abandon her existence to his (Chapter 35).

These various repressive forces overlap, pulling in contrary directions where they do. For instance, her Lowood and Gateshead experiences would suppress her passions, whereas Rochester encourages them. But this too is 'repressive', or rather it would be if at this stage she let herself be shaped by Rochester's will. To yield would be to fit herself to the conventional feminine role Lowood and Gateshead had earlier forbidden her, much as if, having at last found Prince Charming, Cinderella were now allowed to wear her more fortunate sisters' clothes. Only now they have lost their lustre, as the sad figure of the grown Georgiana, and the unpleasant one of Blanche Ingram, remind us.

Another way of saying this is that for the adult Jane, 'head' and 'heart' are indivisible aspects of the self. We may assume that Jane's central desire is to preserve the unified integrity of her inner being, so that she can be happy in love, both bound to another, yet 'free', with both head and heart satisfied. In the interest of this balance she must lean one way, resisting threats to her passion, or heart, when the threat blows from that quarter, then leaning to the other when the threat is to her independent, thinking self. So in the end it is not a simple matter of passion or repression. Rather these are opposite poles through which Jane must ply her difficult course.

3.5 THE FEMINIST PERSPECTIVE

Charlotte Brontë was very disappointed when her life-long friend Mary Taylor criticised *Jane Eyre* for being soft on the 'rights of woman' issue. The tough-minded Mary argued that equal opportunity in work was the important issue, something she felt strongly about as an independent pioneer in New Zealand. Jane's marriage therefore seemed a crucial evasion.

Recent feminist critics have taken a more lenient view. As they interpret the book, *Jane Eyre* is important less for what it advocates, and more for what it diagnoses regarding the condition of Victorian women. In this respect she is seen as a pioneer. Just as Jane has to battle against repressive forces that would encourage self-destroying conformity, so Charlotte Brontë had to battle against the cultural inhibitions she was brought up with, which would have stifled her voice. The obstacles were numerous. Women writers were so lightly regarded that the Brontës considered it advisable to adopt the 'male' pen names of 'Currer', 'Ellis' and 'Acton'. Female sexuality was a secretive topic made worse by the period's preference for euphemism and sentimentality. And perhaps most seriously of all, Charlotte Brontë had no English, certainly no respectable, literary model to copy, no writer in whose footsteps she could safely follow. If Jane had to speak the unspeakable by confessing her desire to herself, Charlotte Brontë had to write the 'unwritten'. This meant adopting old methods to new purposes. In looking back at our discussion of the red-room episode, one might fairly ask if Charlotte Brontë could have possibly meant such a profusion of sexual reference. But the 'feminist' response would be that when conventional language is silent, 'symbolic' means are necessary. When society is reticent, art must be indirect. The imagery of the red-room might only offer tenuous hints, but given Charlotte Brontë's cultural situation, tenuous hints are all one can expect.

The attraction of the 'feminist case' is that it helps make sense of a great deal of the book that might seem so much melodramatic nonsense, such as Mrs Rochester being locked away in the attic, the attempted murders, cries in the night, strange coincidences, the beastliness of Blanche Ingram, the brooding oddness of Rochester, the excessive coldness of St John. All these elements are part of the novel's Gothic strain (see Section 4.5 below). The feminist argument is that it is through the Gothic characters, events and imagery that Charlotte Brontë articulates the 'unwritten', giving voice to the otherwise unexpressed. The contrary argument is that this is making a lot out of very little, and that in any event it foists a twentieth-century concern on to a nineteenth-century text. The feminist response would then be that giving voice to the feminine experience was indeed a pressing nineteenth-century concern for women.

It would be wrong to ask 'is the feminist argument right?' The question should rather be 'does it help us understand *Jane Eyre* better?' The 'feminist case' is very involved, and the material provided here (in Section 2.2 above, and Sections 4.5 and 4.6 below) should be thought of only as a rudimentary sketch. Even so, you should have enough of this controversial 'case' to ask whether it helps you read *Jane Eyre* better.

4 TECHNICAL FEATURES

4.1 THE NOVEL OF MANNERS

The last century was a flourishing period for the novel, with many great books written in a wide variety of styles. Even so, the 'strand' that particularly stands out is the 'novel of manners', in which realistically rendered characters are set in a closely observed society. Jane Austen (1775–1817) and George Eliot (1819–1890) are good examples. The brilliant realism of these novels makes it easy to 'live' in their alien worlds, as if an inhabitant. *Jane Eyre* is such a novel in that it too creates a captivating world, but it is also true to say that Charlotte Brontë was not altogether happy with this style of novel writing.

Charlotte Brontë's discomfort with the novel of manners, as represented by Jane Austen, is evident in her letters, although at times she could happily approve of the earlier writer's craftsmanship. She tells the critic G. H. Lewes, that in *Pride and Prejudice* Jane Austen 'exquisitely adapts her means to her end: both are very subdued, a little contracted, but never absurd'. Much later in her career, Charlotte Brontë confessed to her publisher that she had read *Emma* 'with just the degree of admiration which Miss Austen herself would have thought sensible and suitable'. But then the complaint: '[T]here is a Chinese Fidelity, a miniature delicacy in the painting: she ruffles her reader by nothing vehement, disturbs him by nothing profound: the Passions are perfectly unknown to her; she rejects even a speaking acquaintance with that stormy Sisterhood . . . Her business is not half so much with the human heart as with the human eyes, mouth, hands and feet.' She rounds off with the 'heresy' that Jane Austen was 'insensible', meaning somewhat impervious to passion.

These remarks may not tell us a great deal about Jane Austen, but they do tell us a great deal about Charlotte Brontë and how she viewed the proper business of the novel. She may have admired Jane Austen's craftsmanship, but for her, there was always something lacking. Jane Austen was not 'great' because she lacked 'poetry'; she is 'shrewd and observant', but not 'sagacious and profound'. Jane Austen's 'ladies and gentlemen, in their elegant but confined houses', were in the end, for her purposes, dismal and claustrophobic. Such comments gain in meaning when we consider that the novel of manners is primarily a novel of judgement, of refined moral perception. In *Pride and Prejudice* Elizabeth Bennet discovers that prejudice has clouded her judgement, an embarrassing discovery as she had prided herself on the clarity of her views. In *Emma* the heroine learns that her 'harmless' penchant for matchmaking is really an abuse of her social position, and that Mr Knightley exemplifies the truly responsible role. In both these novels – and in several others of Jane Austen's – the heroines undergo a process of self-discovery, of learning more about themselves, the society they live in, and the true nature of their obligations to both. Charlotte Brontë had not read Jane Austen until after writing *Jane Eyre*, but in comparing her way of rendering her heroine's development with Jane Austen's, she clearly did not find excessive similarity in Jane Austen's method. The salient points of Jane Eyre's development were not to be rendered exclusively through a close observation of Jane's progress in moral judgements; rather these points were to be found among the 'stormy Sisterhood' of passions, and required 'poetry' to express them. If Jane Austen was not 'sagacious and profound', she herself was, or so she hoped. 'Profound' is often used as a purely emotive word meaning 'good'; but in Charlotte Brontë's case we can take it to mean that which is hidden, and at the foundation of character. Consequently, other than 'traditional' means were required to express character – hence the 'poetry' of her work, and her reliance on symbol, imagery and metaphor.

This is not to say that *Jane Eyre* has no points of comparison with the 'traditional' novel. To the contrary, there are many such points. An impulse towards realism was a dominating feature of the school of novel writing represented by Jane Austen, George Eliot and Henry James, a realism typified by these writers' ability to create characters with great psychological probability. One can fairly say that they create personalities that 'leave the page'; at any rate, it is not hard to think or talk of characters such as Emma Woodhouse, Dorothea Brooke or Isabel Archer as if they were 'real'. This illusion of reality is usually created by having the characters react differently in the differing social circumstances in which they find themselves. A character who always behaves the same appears to have no distinctive psychology, but one that responds anew to changing circumstances gives the illusion of having a mind, a personality, a psychology. In interpreting these characters we try to deduce the motives that impel their behaviour. We try to read their character. This is exactly true of a great deal of *Jane Eyre*, but as we shall also see, this is not the full extent of Charlotte Brontë's means of telling us about her characters.

4.2 CHARACTERISATION

Jane Eyre

We learn a great deal about Jane's character through the company she keeps and her manner of response. At Gateshead we learn that Jane is impulsive, but also sullen and withdrawn. She is frightened and miserable, but also spirited. At times her anger and resentment cause her to flash out at her antagonists, but at Lowood a different side of her character is revealed, a desire to be loved. Treated kindly, she softens, repaying the love shown to her with interest. Even so, her anger and resentment persist. She is unable to follow Helen Burns's example, and forgive those who torment her. Leaving Lowood reveals a spirit of independence and determination, together with a practical understanding of her situation. Although impulsive, she is not headstrong. To the contrary, she is able to reflect sensibly on her future. Her character development continues at Thornfield. We see that she is capable of turning a tactful and sympathetic face to the world. She is kind to Mrs Fairfax, and endeavours to befriend Adèle while sincerely working in her charge's best interest. But if she is politely sensitive, she is not unduly deferential, and from the beginning she refuses to be cowed by Rochester's frequently over-bearing character; indeed, she is capable of giving as good as she gets. Her principal weapon is a wry sense of irony, and a refusal to take others beyond how she finds them. She is not easily seduced or intimidated by class. But Jane's irony is also a defence, a means of keeping her deepest feelings hidden from a potentially hostile world and, at times, even from herself. As she gains in trust, she gains in directness; but once again she is capable of asserting herself if challenged or abused, as witnessed by the contempt she reserves for Blanche Ingram and her circle. As we have already seen in the episode of the disastrous 'wedding', she has great inner resources of strength and determination, and is able to command herself to do what she feels is right in spite of the sorest of temptations. This inner strength supports her through her trial on the moors, and is again manifest in her refusal of St John. The even division of her legacy reveals her enduring generosity of spirit, as well as a continuing need for a loving family.

Rochester

As we read Jane's character from the way she responds to her changing circumstances, so we read the others. As is intimated from the beginning, Rochester is burdened down by a secret guilt, and this makes him untrusting, fractious, contradictory and perverse. He is imperious and direct, and is clearly used to wielding his social power. But we gain glimpses into a hidden vulnerability by his sudden tendernesses and solicitude. He may wish to appear hard, but as Jane's intuition early on informs us, there is an inner fund of warmth and generosity. Even so, he is frequently cruel and, as it seems, callous. With Blanche and her friends he appears a perfectly thoughtless member of the ruling classes, an impression strengthened by his apparent disregard for Jane's feelings. But always the man reveals himself beneath the bluster. He has an apparent cavalier disregard for Adèle, but buys her presents, and sees to her future; Jane appears forgotten, but then is thoughtfully introduced.

As the book progresses the reader is brought ever closer to the mystery that explains this enigmatic behaviour, and at the moment of final revelation, the inconsistencies melt away. Disillusioned with society, with the hypocrisy of his class and, as he sees it, the stupidity of its conventions, he has sunk into misanthropic isolation, embittered by the frustration of his impulse to love. Jane appears as the entire, vital human being with whom he feels he can find a satisfying union. Not daring to hope, he places obstacles in Jane's way, as if to test her; finding her succeed, he warms towards her, but then pulls back, either because he fears society will meddle, thus destroying his dream, or because of a sudden smiting of unworthiness, or a general disbelief in the chances of success. Finally determined, he grasps his opportunity with both hands. But all along there is an egotism in his behaviour, a self-centredness revealed in his lack of candidness towards Jane, and by his desire to possess her on his terms (an attitude best exemplified by his wish to dress Jane as he wishes, and not as she does). Still, however imperious he might appear, the depth of his devotion to Jane is clearly attested to by his long vigil outside her door, while the final heroism of his character is displayed in his heedless bid to save his wife, terrible millstone though she is. At the end we see a Rochester mollified by love and repentance, his domineering egotism softened, as if adversity has proved a crucible, with the outward dross of his character melted away.

St John Rivers

St John Rivers's character is by comparison displayed rather than revealed; that is to say, we learn more from what he says than from what he does. But here the sketching of character is quickened by the similarities he bears to Jane. Knowing her, we know him. He shares Jane's history of social frustration. They are both hot, passionate characters in that they have strong, assertive selves. But whereas Jane's character is regulated by the naturalising channel of love opened through her connection with Rochester, St John's follows a more devious course. With no direct outlet for his ambition, he chooses the indirect one of a self-sacrificing missionary. As a consequence he is tragically 'denatured'. Although passionate by instinct, fortune has made him cold and hard, the repression of desire exacting its costs.

Minor characters

The remaining characters, by and large, are only lightly sketched in. Moreover they do not change as their circumstances do: Mrs Reed, her children, the Rivers sisters, Helen Burns or Miss Temple do not surprise us with some unexpected reaction. To the contrary, they are highly predictable.

Such characters are usually referred to as 'flat' (Jane and Rochester, by comparison, as 'round'). It was the theory of the American writer, Henry James (1843–1916), that such flat characters are necessary to flesh out aspects of the 'round' ones. They were part of the economy of the novel form in which a central character could be succinctly elaborated through the parallels and contrasts afforded by the 'flat' characters (it is worth noting that the flat characters, such as Helen and Miss Temple, who parallel aspects of Jane are idealised, while those contrasting with her, such as Georgiana and Blanche, are grotesque). Even so, such flat characters were to tally with psychological probability. But when Elizabeth Rigby complained, in the Quarterly Review, that Charlotte Brontë's portrayal of high society at Thornfield bore no relationship to any society she knew, she had a point, and it was not that Charlotte Brontë was incapable of creating realistic characters.

Rather we should notice that besides their narrative and social functions, the flat characters in Jane Eyre have a symbolic function which often overrides the need for social verisimilitude. This is foremost a question of genre (see Section 4.4 below). As characters in a realistically observed social setting, that is to say, as characters in a novel of manners, they should conform to the reader's sense of the 'probable and ordinary'. But as characters in a 'romance' they may serve as symbolic foils to the main character, thus helping to bring out a hidden aspect of the principal character's psyche.

Georgiana and Eliza provide examples. As we have seen, Georgiana does not 'grow up', and the petulant doll-like qualities that were cute in the child show badly in the adult. Eliza is also selfish, although hers is spiritual rather than worldly pride. With their exaggerated qualities these figures may not be entirely realistic. Indeed, Jane herself comments on their allegorical nature, the one being 'feeling without judgement', the other 'judgement untempered by feeling' (Chapter 21). Jane has both generous feeling and rigorous judgement, so in these respects at least the two cousins externalise aspects of Jane's character; or, perhaps more accurately, they underline how these two aspects, which are split among themselves, are united in Jane. The cousins also help fill in the thematic background to Jane's choices. When she feels inclined to say 'yes' to Rochester the first time, to abandon herself to feeling without judgement, there is the grim spectre of Georgiana; and when St John proposes, there is Eliza.

Blanche Ingram is another example. At the time she appears in the novel, Jane is struggling with her passion. Jane notices Miss Ingram's 'low brow' and 'high features', which are generally indicative of her character (Chapter 17). Although physically superb, she is spiritually and intellectually shallow. It was no doubt the exaggerated fineness of Blanche's person, and the excessive grossness of her manners, that Elizabeth Rigby objected to. But these very excesses help make the contrast with Jane. One way of describing Blanche is that she is the woman without scruples or morality. Rochester is soon to ask Jane to break with her scruples. So Blanche too may be said to represent a possibility for Jane's development. As Jane considers following her passion and not her judgement, Blanche Ingram joins Georgiana in casting a warning shadow.

The tendency of 'flat' characters to assume a symbolic function is typical of the other narrative tradition Charlotte Brontë called upon, Gothic romance. Whereas the novel endeavours to give us a picture of society, romance serves to illuminate the characters' inner reality, hidden and obscure. At the time of writing, the current taste in fiction was for works that captured the feel of contemporary life, as in the works of Mrs Gaskell (1810–65), which were both panoramic and minute, or in the comic manner of Thackeray (1811–63) and Dickens (1812–70), which depicted life in the capital in its bustling, vital diversity. But in *Jane Eyre* Charlotte Brontë turned to Gothic romance, a form that had experienced its heyday fifty years earlier, in the 1790s. With its gloomy castles, stormy weather, moonlit landscapes, its tormented heroes and heroines, dreams and portents, plot involutions and mysteries, and above all with its passionate love interests, the Gothic romance may have seemed a relic of an earlier, simpler era. Where her contemporaries favoured the tenacious complications of the present, Charlotte Brontë brought simplifying fantasy. Or so it might seem. But the real measure of her achievement is that she turned Gothic decor into usable symbolism. It is here in particular that she 'writes the unwritten' by renewing an old form. Accordingly, in understanding any of *Jane Eyre*'s characters, we must not only attend to the implications of their behaviour, but to the implications of the imagery (see Sections 4.5 and 4.6 below).

4.3 POINT OF VIEW

Choice of point of view is one of the most crucial decisions any novelist takes, and that is because point of view determines the manner in which the story is told, which in turn influences the experience of the book and its meaning. In this section we will be examining the various consequences of Charlotte Brontë's choice.

In adopting a first person narrative stance, rather than the more familiar third, Charlotte Brontë broke ranks with the majority of her contemporaries. The third person, or 'omniscient narrator', leads a reader to expect an objective view of the book's characters. It gives solidity to events, as if a true history were unfolding before our eyes. Not only do we see characters as they see themselves, but we see them as others do, and this too lends a steadying perspective. The first person, on the other hand, magnifies the central character. We are, as it were, swallowed up in their world. The problem then becomes whether or not we can trust this narrator. Is the narrator reliable? Can we believe what we have been told? Or is the narrative 'distorted' by the narrator's desire to make a good impression, to conceal sensitive issues from the reader? Has he (or she) allowed his emotions to prejudice his story and, in any event, is he in full possession of the facts, regarding himself as well as others?

These same questions are at work in *Jane Eyre*, with the result that we cannot take what Jane tells us at face value. Jane herself informs us of this. Relating her history to Miss Temple, Jane is mindful of Helen's 'warnings against the indulgence of resentment'. Accordingly she infuses her narrative with less 'gall and wormwood' than was usual (Chapter 8). So the possibility arises that elsewhere she is less restrained, and that she lets resentment 'distort' her narrative, thus making it less than 'objective'.

Jane's hint instructs us in the care we need to take as readers. This is especially so given the 'double perspective' of Jane's narrative. The novel begins on a dreary November day when Jane is ten, but is told ten years after her marriage when she is thirty. This makes the narrative *retrospective*. That is to say, she recounts her past with the benefit of hindsight, or through the eyes of the adult. But in doing so she is often swept back into the past, and relates events as if she were in the middle of them, or through the eyes of the child, thus giving us the double perspective of child and adult. Sifting through the evidence provided by this double perspective is crucial to the process of interpreting the novel. Moreover, we the readers are kept guessing in that we are often left uncertain as to whether what we read is an 'adult' perspective we should approve, or a 'childish' one we should deplore.

The reader is drawn into the moral indecisions of the book in other ways as well. As we have seen in Section 3.2, a thematic tension works between the claims of the child and the necessary compromises of the adult. So even when Jane is apparently giving us the full benefit of her hindsight, the correctness of her views is open to question. She might tell us it was wiser to conform, but the reader may want to disagree. Settling into school-teaching at Morton she recalls the 'delusive bliss' she might have had with Rochester in the south of France, instead of being, as she now is, socially useful in Yorkshire. 'Yes; I feel now that I was right when I adhered to principle and law, and scorned and crushed the insane promptings of a frenzied moment' (Chapter 31). But when the legacy rescues her, the vision of social usefulness falls away, and she quits her job. Her celebration of teaching may now seem a hollow attempt at making her lot seem better; was her retrospective support of her rejection of Rochester similarly 'hollow'? If so, why does she say she was right to spurn Rochester in such morally vehement language? Does this tell us something about Jane's psychology, that she has to use strong language because her desire for Rochester is still strong, much as there is no smoke without fire? Once we suspect the reliability of the narrator – that is to say, once we no longer believe the character is a mouthpiece of the author – such questions become fair game.

Another example of Charlotte Brontë's technique of throwing doubt into the mind of the reader occurs in Chapter 23. Jane and Rochester are strolling in the garden in the evening light, with Jane uncomfortably aware that it is wrong to do so. She confidently tells us that it is one of her faults, that although her tongue is usually prompt, it frequently fails at a moment of crisis when a polite excuse is needed to extricate herself from danger. This proves just such a moment.

Jane is aware of the 'evil' of remaining, and says nothing. At this
point we know how much Jane loves Rochester. Is Jane fibbing? Is
this business about a tendency to mental lapses Jane's way of
excusing her desire to remain? If so, then even in retrospect Jane has
difficulty in owning the existence of her desire.

Yet another way of viewing this episode emerges when we recall
the terms of the fiction. Jane is here ostensibly telling a public
audience many of the most intimate details of her private life. Is Jane
trying to excuse herself before this public by inventing a pretext for
staying, thus anticipating the accusation that she led Rochester on? Is
Jane being pressured by social norms, so that she retrospectively fits
her history to the moral standards of her 'reading public'? What both
these interpretations amount to is seeing Jane *dramatically*, as a
character whose utterances may reveal something about her that is
not immediately obvious. In other words, we have to take what Jane
tells us with a pinch of salt.

To sum up, we can identify various kinds of inference arising out of
Charlotte Brontë's subtle use of the first person. First, as we saw, the
use of first person means that anything the narrator tells us *may* be
unreliable due to her 'subjective' involvement. Second, because the
novel involves a process of education which implicates many themes,
the reader is left weighing the child's view against the adult's; that is
to say, the 'double perspective' leaves open the question 'who is
right?' Third, the character's opinions may not be those of the author
at all, but are there to cast light on the character's psychology.
Finally, we may have to make an allowance for a tendency on Jane's
part to fit her history to the expectations of her ostensible 'reading
public'.

These entanglements would seem to require critical vigilance, but a
book is likely to receive it only if it is capable of absorbing our
interest and providing enjoyment, which *Jane Eyre* emphatically
does. *Jane Eyre* absorbs because of its plot, but the forcefulness of
plot is not simply drawn from exciting action, of maddening delay
followed by release. Plots often draw their power from deeper
sources, from what might be called 'collective wishes', and this is
particularly true of 'romance', on which Charlotte Brontë draws.

4.4   REALISM AND ROMANCE

One reason why *Jane Eyre*'s plot is so gripping is that it is a powerful
love story. It is also a 'romance' in the manner of *Cinderella*, where
wishes come true. Jane begins poor and lonely, but ends rich and

loved. The 'family romance' is also typical of fairytales, and this too is present in *Jane Eyre*.

The general structure of the family romance is for an orphan to find his or her parents, or parent substitutes, or a child's bad or adopted family to be replaced by an ideal one, such as in Dickens's *Oliver Twist*. *Jane Eyre* follows a similar pattern, with the ideal Rivers replacing the horrible Reeds as Jane's family. *Jane Eyre* is thus really two romances in one. The episodes at Gateshead, Lowood and Morton are primarily concerned with the family romance, with the Rivers replacing the Reeds, while the events at Thornfield and Ferndean involve the love romance.

The wishes involved here – for an ideal family or loved one – are of a deep-rooted kind, and this makes *Jane Eyre* easy to identify with. But many other fictional works involve similar material without anything like *Jane Eyre*'s power to engage. Clearly other factors are at work.

The most significant factor, perhaps, is Charlotte Brontë's ability to marry romance with realism. This is evident in the way she uses the first person to create vivid environments. 'There was no possibility of taking a walk that day.' From these first words we are plunged into a minutely depicted world in which warm, intimate spaces are contrasted with exposed, cold ones, as, for instance, the red window-seat and the drizzly November day.

This marriage of realism and romance is evident again in the obstacles Charlotte Brontë places in Jane's path. The Reeds and Brocklehurst are so odious that it is hard not to join in with Jane in hating them, just as one hates the villains in *Cinderella*, Westerns, or other romances. But as the novel progresses Jane's antagonists become less exaggerated, and more 'real', with the hideous Reeds and Brocklehurst giving way to the merely obnoxious Ingrams, who in turn yield to St John, who is subtly rather than overtly Jane's antagonist.

We should think of romance as deep wishes triumphantly fulfilled, but also as an overcoming of great adversity. As we have seen, this romance element of desire and threat is reflected in the warm domestic interiors which tantalise Jane. These detailed settings make for realism, as do the obstacles Jane must overcome. As discussed in Section 4.2 above, the illusion of personality in fiction depends upon characters changing with their circumstances. Jane changes as she learns, and as she confronts antagonists, and this heightens her realism as a character.

Jane Eyre's power would thus seem to derive from its balance of realism and romance. 'Romance' infuses universal human emotion into the novel, while the realistic surface makes the action believable. It is possible to argue, however, that these two elements are not always evenly joined. With the possible exceptions of Rochester and St John, the good characters are obviously good, and the bad obviously bad. To use the idiom of the Western, they wear white and black hats. This is an aspect of romance, as are the amazing coincidences, such as Jane's mysterious arrival at her cousins' house. In terms of romance this is perfectly acceptable, for as a structure of desire fulfilled, romance is inherently optimistic. There may be some local difficulty, in which the good are temporarily down and the bad up, but in the long run there is no mistake, and the good and bad return to their proper places. In seeing to this restoration of order, realities are not allowed to intrude, and little concern is shown for logical causality. These features obviously conflict with the conventions of realism, which demand that characters should not be unequivocally good or evil, and that probability be respected. One might censure *Jane Eyre* for this, but perhaps a more liberal view might be to say that as *genres*, 'romance' and 'realism' each say things the other cannot, and in this respect the novel is entitled to have it both ways.

4.5 THE GOTHIC

As mentioned in Section 4.2, the Gothic novel was the variety of romance writing favoured by Charlotte Brontë. The Gothic novel had reached the height of its popularity fifty years earlier, during the 1790s, so we need to think of *Jane Eyre* as belonging to the 'sophisticated' Gothic. That is to say, Charlotte Brontë built on the achievement of earlier writers, an aspect of *Jane Eyre* most evident in Charlotte Brontë's adaptation of Gothic conventions.

The English writer, Ann Radcliffe (1764–1823), was perhaps the most influential figure in setting the *genre*'s pattern. *The Romance of the Forest* (1791), *The Mysteries of Udolpho* (1794) and *The Italian* (1797) were all important and popular works. Typically, a beautiful young woman would be abducted and threatened with seduction, or worse. The plot would therefore move from the pastoral tranquillity of the parental home, to the threatening environment of the brigand's castle. Meanwhile, the girl's lover – infallibly a nice young man of unimpeachable family – endeavours to rescue her, which he does after many trials. Modern feminist critics have interpreted this plot as a resonant 'myth' expressing contemporary female anxieties. In this respect they have turned the tables on the traditional complaint that

Gothic romance was fantasy, by saying that it is fantasy, and very telling because of it.

The freedom of middle-class women was curtailed during the era of the Gothic novel, and nowhere was this more true than marriage, then often a means of commercial exchange, of improving fortunes, or securing futures. In these circumstances a woman's commodity value depended on her sexual purity, which is why Elizabeth Bennet's family, in Jane Austen's *Pride and Prejudice* (1813), are so anxious to ensure that Wickham marries Lydia after he has eloped with her, even though he is a very poor catch. Shop-soiled goods did not have much value on the market. Lydia had to be saved.

At the time of the catastrophe Elizabeth Bennet blames her mother for not imposing stricter limits, and this was frequently the case for unmarried women. They would be kept securely at home, or if let out, under strict guard. With intimacy difficult, and many attachments virtually arranged, marriage must present itself as an alluring and terrifying prospect. As the only means of personal fulfilment offered by society, marriage held obvious attractions; but restricted in choice and opportunity in courtship, it was also a frightening step into the unknown. Ann Radcliffe's Gothic plot would seem to play out this ambivalence. From the perspective of female fear, marriage might seem a ravishing from home, and the future husband an omnipotent villain. He might also be a provocation to desire; hence, as compensation, the hero who proves his devotion and selfless love for the heroine by his unstinting efforts to save her. In this respect the Gothic plot both recognises female desire and repudiates it. The villain is overtly masculine, aggressive, potent, and darkly attractive; the hero, by contrast, is 'nice', young, conventional, and impelled by disinterested love rather than rapacious lust. The heroine inevitably prefers the hero, the boy next door rather than the rake up the street.

Jane Eyre is embroiled in this plot, but with significant inversions. Jane is not abducted to Thornfield, but goes there of her own volition. She is naturally unaware of the existence of Rochester, but the plot is still importantly different in that Jane is active rather than passive. She does not wait to be acted upon, as do Ann Radcliffe's heroines; to the contrary, she sets out to seek her fortune, thus adopting the conventional male role.

We find another modification of the Radcliffe plot in the presentation of Thornfield, or rather there is a blending of two different motifs, one taken from the novel of manners, the other from the Gothic novel. Houses are important in fiction as they generally reflect the characters of the people who live in them. As we have seen, in the Gothic plot the movement is from the parental home to the abductor's, and back again – from a pastoral home signifying tranquillity, to the villain's remote and threatening castle, from which the heroine is rescued. In the novel of manners, however, the movement is often the 'comic' one of moving from a troubled or restrictive home to the lover's harmonious one, a move effected by marriage. Mr Knightley in Jane Austen's *Emma* is a perfect example. His home, a country mansion called Donwell Abbey, is the image of harmony; it fits into the landscape, as if growing out of it, and is perfectly adapted to the society in which it is situated. As such it suggests Mr Knightley's idealised character while also underlining the social harmony of the different classes who live in happy and fruitful proximity. Knightley is a member of the gentry, and is a model of his kind, considerate alike of the landscape and those who depend upon him, and all this is expressed by Donwell Abbey. On the face of it Thornfield is such a house, and as such it holds out the promise of a comic ending in which the principal protagonists will marry, and harmony will be restored at all levels. But the house has another face which Jane discovers on her tour of inspection, a Gothic side represented by the ancient heart of the building with its gloomy recesses, mysterious passages, and hidden attics. It is worth reading Chapter 11 again to see how Charlotte Brontë manages the shift in presentation, from an image of inviting social harmony, to one of Gothic threat and disturbance. If Rochester's house is two-sided, so apparently is his character: like his house he presents a conventional, gentrified front to the public, while concealing an inner core of guilt and disquiet. The presentation of Thornfield thus deepens our understanding of Rochester through its suggestion of a link. It also advances the plot. The difference in rank and wealth are the most obvious obstacles to Jane's and Rochester's union, but now another emerges, the Gothic blemishes in Rochester's character. Both must be confronted and vanquished before the resolution can occur.

Thornfield, then, is an ambivalent image of home as site of comic resolution, of domestic bliss, and home as threatening castle. At this stage Charlotte Brontë draws upon another potent cultural myth to advance her thinking. Completing her inspection of Thornfield's upper storey, Jane remarks that a long attic corridor, with its shut up doors, looks to her like 'some Bluebeard's castle' (Chapter 11). In the original story a young girl is married to Bluebeard, who is rich and lives in a castle. He warns her not to open a certain door,but curiosity overcomes her, and as soon as she can, she does, making a very grisly discovery in the process – the butchered remains of Bluebeard's seven previous wives.

Rochester, of course, does not have seven dead wives locked away, just one mad one, but by alluding to the Bluebeard myth Charlotte Brontë is able to enlarge upon her theme. In the original story the fear of marriage is magnified to the fear of literal death; in touching it the novel now suggests that Jane shares this fear. Rochester's desire is a potent, possibly destroying force; that is the threat the Gothic aspect of Thornfield portends, and it is something with which both characters must come to terms. Charlotte Brontë brings the myth within the confines of realism by making the original Mrs Rochester mad rather than butchered. Murder might not be a plausible threat, but being shut up in an attic in the master's house has its believable symbolism. Rochester says that Jane is an angel and wants to clip her to his wrist; and from a spirited woman's point of view this might very well seem a stifling, soul-destroying threat. To give in, and play the part of an 'angel', is itself a kind of captivity, or destruction.

The intertwining of literary models now takes another twist. As her threatening abductors with their gloomy castles attest, Ann Radcliffe incorporated the Bluebeard myth when making her Gothic plot. Her villainous 'Bluebeard' figure in turn influenced the hero fashioned by the English Romantic poet, Lord Byron (1788–1824). The 'Byronic hero' became an enormously influential stereotype. Unconventionally handsome, saturnine and taciturn, he was usually an outcast from civilised society, and burdened down with an obscure curse. 'Mad, bad, and dangerous to know' was a popular description of Byron, and the same could be said of his hero. Rochester is modelled on this Byronic figure. In Chapter 14 Rochester lifts up his 'sable locks' to reveal an intellectual brow, but with 'an abrupt deficiency where the suave signs of benevolence should have risen'. Although the Byronic hero conceals a feeling heart, he is not 'nice'. Rochester reveals another typical Byronic feature in having roamed the world in dissatisfied search, and, most significantly of all, in being 'hampered, burdened, cursed' (Chapter 14).

By drawing upon the Byronic hero Charlotte Brontë was able to enrich her plot while deepening Rochester's character. Again, the point was to enlarge upon Jane's sexual aggressiveness; where the Radcliffe villain is only latently attractive, Rochester is straightforwardly, if unconventionally, so. He is sexually compelling, as Jane happily admits. Whereas sexual attraction is left menacingly in the background of the traditional Radcliffe novel, it is brought centre stage in *Jane Eyre*. Jane does not crumble before this potent figure, as a Radcliffe heroine would, nor does she expect a saviour to the rescue. St John Rivers may be said to fulfil this aspect of the plot in that he offers an alternative to Rochester, and in many ways he is an exaggeration of the conventional piety the Radcliffe hero has to offer. Charlotte Brontë adapts the alternatives of the Gothic plot, drawing out the sexuality of the 'villain' and the orthodoxy of the 'hero'. Accordingly, her focus shifts from female sexual terror to a consideration of female desire; or rather, Jane is an equal combatant in the battle of sexual wills. Rather than someone who is fought over, she does her own fighting, and much of the unconventional force of the novel derives from this.

4.6 TEXTUAL FEATURES

So far we have noted that *Jane Eyre* has its feet in two different camps of the novel – in the novel of manners, which endeavours to portray believable characters in realistic settings, and romance, which is frequently improbable, with strange twists and turns, mysterious characters, and odd images and symbols. In this section we will further investigate *Jane Eyre*'s romance qualities, in particular the characters, images and symbols which repeat themselves, and which, in so doing, create new thematic patterns. In particular we will be looking at repetitions of character, imagery and incident.

At the beginning of Chapter 21 Jane tells us that she has dreamt of a fractious baby on seven successive nights: 'I did not like this iteration of one idea – this strange recurrence of one image.' Jane tells us that the superstitious Bessie believed these recurring dreams to be portents, but we should see such recurrences as clues. Redness, blood and fire form one recurring image cluster, while ice, snow and whiteness form another, oppositional one. This image antithesis is present from the first chapter, where Jane sits in the window-seat, enfolded in scarlet drapery, looking out on a bleak November scene. The red-room offers further elaboration in that it is both sumptuous and scarlet, chill and icy. This early antithesis is then 'iterated' later on in the figures of Jane's two suitors. When Jane first meets Rochester at home, the fire shines 'full on his face'. The association of fire and redness with sexual passion, ironically, is most fully expressed by St John, who pictures himself in a kind of Turkish red-room, with Rosamund Oliver smiling at him with 'coral lips'. But this is only a prelude; having suppressed his inclinations, St John has become 'cold' and 'hard' (Chapter 32), and later, echoing Brockle-hurst's 'black pillar', a 'cold cumbrous column' (Chapter 34).

Jane's essential character, then, is associated with fire and burn-ing – she is, as Rochester says of her, 'a soul made of fire' (Chapter 24). While she more demurely tells us that she feels passion, or loves

Rochester, the imagery reveals her as being 'consumed' by desire, thus bringing alive what is otherwise a dead metaphor (being 'burned' by passion). The imagery thus instructs us as to the nature of the twin dangers that threaten her development, either of being consumed by unrestrained passion, or being doused, or frozen, by repression. In this respect the image of antithesis of fire and ice introduced at the beginning of the novel equips us with a way of following Jane's development as the action progresses. The recurring imagery also helps us spot her deepest affinities. Rochester, too, is a character of fire, so her deepest affinity is clearly with him, and not the icy St John.

Another strangely recurring image is the moon, mysteriously present at nearly every moment of crisis in Jane's life. It glimmers outside the red-room, bathes Jane and Helen the night Helen dies, and lights up Rochester's approach on horseback. The night of Bertha Mason's second attack is lit by the rising moon, as is the evening on which Rochester proposes; it is there when Jane decides to leave Thornfield, and then again when she renounces St John. The moon is so omnipresent that one might be inclined to dismiss it as Gothic decor, but then Jane is insistent that it has a specific meaning for her. On the 'worst night of her life', when she decides to flee from Rochester, the moon bursts from behind a cloud in the shape of a 'white human form' shining in the azure, 'inclining a glorious brow earthward'. It whispers for Jane to flee, to which Jane answers, 'Mother, I will' (Chapter 27). The scene recalls an earlier incident when the clear-browed Miss Temple succours Helen and Jane, her entrance swathed in moonlight. So Jane herself sees the moon as an image of the feminine ideal patterened out on Miss Temple; that is to say, as the spirit or genius of femininity. As an image the moon need not be sqeezed to so narrow a referent; it is rather an index of change, and a token of Jane's inner nature to which she endeavours to be faithful. Variations in Jane's emotional states seem to be registered by changes in the moon. But the moon also appears as a guardian for which Jane feels an instinctive affinity.

Thus we see that the purpose of these strange recurrences is to alert us to much that is happening beneath the surface of the action. Jane's development is from childhood to maturity, and represents an education, a gaining of wisdom. In this respect the choices she makes between selfish and social needs, feeling and principle, passion and judgement, are all important; but the recurring, 'obsessive' images of moon, fire and redness also 'hint' at another, complementary, development, in which Jane comes to terms with conflicting aspects of her nature.

The repetition or doubling of character is important here. As we have seen, in *Jane Eyre* many of the characters mirror or echo each other, and many of the minor characters help exemplify differing aspects of the central one (see Section 4.2). This device is central to the expression of Jane's 'secret development'. The most important examples are Helen Burns and Bertha Mason, who apparently represent different aspects of Jane.

Another way of saying this is that Helen and Bertha are Jane's *alter egos*. This was an implicit aspect of the Gothic, and here once again Charlotte Brontë adapts the form by making the hidden explicit. As we learn, Helen and Bertha are not simply aspects of Jane, they are contradictory aspects. As mentioned earlier, Helen is linked to Jane through the imagery of fire, of 'burning'. She signifies passion, but a passion internalised into religious ecstasy, or as it is now said, 'sublimated'. Jane, too, is prone to such 'sublimation', as we see at the end where she nearly gives in to St John's ecstatic vision of self-sacrifice (a vision at which Helen would not have hesitated). But as the example of Helen has already alerted us, a choice such as this is no choice at all; as with Helen, it signifies a destructive self-denial.

Thus, if Helen represents passion sublimated into conscience, or religious duty, Bertha Mason represents passion unrestrained. What is suppressed in Helen, is uncontrollable in Bertha. In this respect it is interesting to compare the fire imagery associated with each. Helen only takes fire in the presence of Miss Temple. Her 'kindled' powers light up her features, giving her cheeks and eyes a glowing, shining 'radiance', so that her 'soul sat on her lips' (Chapter 8). Helen's inner 'fire' only occasionally shows, and then as an eloquent 'discourse'; the pyromaniac Bertha, conversely, cannot resist the impulse to light fires.

Whether Bertha's compulsion means anything here is perhaps uncertain, but it does hold some interest in the light of Bertha's madness, which, as Rochester makes abundantly clear in Chapter 27, is nymphomania. He might call it 'debauchery', or circumspectly refer to the agonies of shame she inflicted upon him, but all doubt is dispelled when he calls her his 'Indian Messalina', Messalina being the notorious wife of the Roman Emperor Claudius who scandalised Rome with her prodigious intemperance. Interestingly, Jane is drawn to the third storey where Bertha is kept, to walk the gallery compulsively, as if answering to some mysterious affinity. This hint of a link between the two of them is strengthened by the timing of Bertha's attacks, which coincide with crises in Jane's relationship with Rochester. Bertha attempts to burn Rochester the night Jane first admits her love; she bites Mason after the gypsy episode in which

Rochester's love for Jane is re-affirmed; and she tears Jane's veil on the eve of the wedding. Whenever Jane's desire for Rochester is inflamed by circumstance, Bertha appears.

According to the theories of Sigmund Freud (1856–1939), the self or ego is caught between the conscience, derived from conventional morality, and the id (literally, the 'it') which is to be thought of as a chaos of unconscious desires knowing no good or evil. There seems to be something of this in *Jane Eyre*, with Jane caught between Helen Burns, who would stand for conscience, and Bertha Mason, who bears a passing resemblance to Freud's image of the libido, or id. This may be pressing the symbolism too far, but it is certainly hard to discount the view that at this stage in her development, Jane is 'split' by contrary inclinations. The imagery thus elaborates a side of Jane's maturation that is otherwise hidden, that her development is not simply a matter of getting her moral priorities right; it is also a psychological matter of finding a balance between conflicting aspects of her character.

Helen Burns and Bertha Mason thus help flesh out the abstract scheme of feeling versus judgement, passion versus conscience. In particular the ideas are developed through the description of personal attributes. Bertha is the literal embodiment of desire, being large, full bodied, sultry and dark. In her madness she is also in a state of slack-mouthed idiocy. Interestingly, Bertha shares a number of attributes with Blanche Ingram, which Rochester himself draws attention to, in Chapter 27, when he says that he found Bertha 'a fine woman, in the style of Blanche Ingram: tall, dark, and majestic'. As we have noted, Blanche Ingram has a 'low brow' (Chapter 17) which would indicate an undeveloped intellect, while Bertha's is that of a 'pigmy', although her 'propensities' are 'giant'. The point of these similarities would seem to be to blacken Blanche with Bertha's descriptive brush, thus emphasising the dehumanising nature of passion without intelligence. That, anyway, is what Jane feels – witness her comments on Mason, whose features are not only an echo of his sister's, but also of Blanche's: they display a 'tame, vacant life . . . there was no thought on the low, even forehead; no command in that blank, brown eye' (Chapter 18). Once again the relationship between judgement and passion is seen to bear a psychological dimension; unrestrained, passion blights the intelligence. Significantly, all the women save Jane find Mason attractive. Given the potential unreliability of Jane's narrative, it is possible to see the descriptions of Blanche and Mason as representing Jane's fears that she has sacrificed her intellect in making an 'idol' of

Rochester. In so far as she fears, she despises, so she may exaggerate the characters who seem to possess the qualities she fears.

Repetitions of relationships are also important. Rochester's spurning of Blanche announces to Jane Rochester's eligibility as a suitor, as it shows that his interests in Jane are not debasing; if he does not want a gorgeous person, then he must want something spiritually better. The proper pattern of a relationship is also implied in that it is the opposite of what Blanche has to offer. This in turn is a repetition of an earlier episode, Rochester's narration of his affair with Céline Varens. Again Rochester's repudiation of Céline signifies Rochester's suitability; but it is only partial. The daughter (Adèle) is a double or repetition of the mother, and by exemplifying Céline through her child, the infantile regressiveness of woman as object is suggested. This in turn gives point to Jane's refusal to knuckle under to Rochester's demands for her to duplicate Céline by dressing in the same fashion (for one thing it would put Jane on a par with Adèle, whom Rochester does dress). If Rochester intellectually knows that he wants a 'soul made of fire' for a wife, and not a Blanche or Céline Varens, he cannot as yet fully act on that knowledge.

Aside from the repetition of aspects of Jane in other characters, we have in other characters' relationships variations of Jane's situations which have instructive value for her, and which enlarge on the book's themes. Blanche and Rochester, St John and Rosamund are the most notable examples. In addition there are other kinds of repetition, such as Jane's recurring dream images, and the images in her paintings. As we have also seen, there are repetitions of situations, such as the two marriage proposals. It is worth your while exploring further what they mean.

Finally, there is a great deal of 'foreshadowing', actions later to be enacted on a larger scale. Jane's helping the injured Rochester on their first meeting echoes their last, with Jane supporting the invalid on both occasions. The charade played out by Rochester and Blanche Ingram with its final, sordid tableau of a ruinous marriage is both an anticipation of an event that does not happen, the marriage between Rochester and Blanche, and an allusion to one that has, Rochester's marriage to Bertha. Enigmatically, Jane dreams of a ruined Thornfield and a fleeing Rochester (Chapter 25). The significance of the chestnut tree blasted on the night Rochester proposes, however, is as clear as the other is obscure.

The direct function of these foreshadowings is to keep the reader guessing: will these premonitions be fulfilled? But this more trivial interest awakens a deeper one, which introduces the reader into the

Gothic mystery and its obscure but telling meanings. In this respect the 'obsessive' iteration of images and figures is significant, but it is important to note that there is no simple one-to-one correspondence between images and ideas. *Jane Eyre* is not a puzzle. They are rather shapes in the background that help give us additional perspectives on more immediate events and themes.

5 SPECIMEN PASSAGE

AND

COMMENTARY

5.1 SPECIMEN PASSAGE

The opening of Chapter 25:

The month of courtship had wasted: its very last hours were being numbered. There was no putting off the day that advanced – the bridal day; and all preparations for its arrival were complete. *I*, at least, had nothing more to do: there were my trunks, packed, locked, corded, ranged in a row along the wall of my little chamber; to-morrow, at this time, they would be far on their road to London: and so should I (*D.V.*) – or rather, not I, but one Jane Rochester, a person whom as yet I knew not. The cards of address alone remained to nail on: they lay, four little squares, in the drawer. Mr Rochester had himself written the direction, 'Mrs Rochester, —— Hotel, London', on each: I could not persuade myself to affix them, or to have them affixed. Mrs Rochester! She did not exist: she would not be born till to-morrow, some time after eight o'clock a.m.; and I would wait to be assured she had come into the world alive before I assigned to her all that property. It was enough that in yonder closet, opposite my dressing-table, garments said to be hers had already displaced my black stuff Lowood frock and straw bonnet: for not to me appertained that suit of wedding raiment; the pearl-coloured robe, the vapoury veil pendent from the usurped portmanteau. I shut the closet to conceal the strange, wraith-like apparel it contained; which, at this evening hour – nine o'clock – gave out certainly a most ghostly shimmer through the shadow of my apartment. 'I will leave you by yourself, white dream,' I said, 'I am feverish: I hear the wind blowing: I will go out of doors and feel it.'

It was not only the hurry of preparation that made me feverish: not only the anticipation of the great change – the new life which was to commence to-morrow: both these circumstances had their share, doubtless, in producing that restless, excited mood which hurried me forth at this late hour into the darkening grounds; but a third cause influenced my mind more than they.

I had at heart a strange and anxious thought. Something had happened which I could not comprehend; no one knew of or had seen the event but myself: it had taken place the preceding night. Mr Rochester that night was absent from home; nor was he yet returned; business had called him to a small estate of two or three farms he possessed thirty miles off - business it was requisite he should settle in person, previous to this meditated departure from England. I waited now his return; eager to disburthen my mind, and to seek of him the solution of the enigma that perplexed me. Stay till he comes, reader; and, when I disclose my secret to him, you shall share the confidence.

I sought the orchard, driven to its shelter by the wind, which all day had blown strong and full from the south, without, however, bringing a speck of rain. Instead of subsiding as night drew on, it seemed to augment its rush and deepen its roar: the trees blew steadfastly one way, never writhing round, and scarcely tossing back their boughs once in an hour; so continuous was the strain bending their branchy heads northwards – the clouds drifted from pole to pole, fast following, mass on mass: no glimpse of blue sky had been visible that July day.

It was not without a certain wild pleasure I ran before the wind, delivering my trouble of mind to the measureless air-torrent thundering through space. Descending the laurel walk, I faced the wreck of the chestnut-tree; it stood up, black and riven: the trunk, split down the centre, gasped ghastly. The cloven halves were not broken from each other, for the firm base and strong roots kept them unsundered below; though community of vitality was destroyed – the sap could flow no more: their great boughs on each side were dead, and next winter's tempests would be sure to fell one or both to earth: as yet, however, they might be said to form one tree – a ruin, but an entire ruin.

'You did right to hold fast to each other,' I said: as if the monster splinters were living things, and could hear me. 'I think, scathed as you look, and charred and scorched, there must be a little sense of life in you yet, rising out of that adhesion at the faithful, honest roots: you will never have green leaves more – never more see birds making nests and singing idylls in your boughs; the time of pleasure and love is over with you; but you are not desolate: each of you has a comrade to sympathize with him in his decay.' As I looked up at them, the moon appeared momentarily in that part of the sky which filled their fissure; her disc was blood-red and half overcast; she seemed to throw on me one bewildered, dreary glance, and buried herself again instantly in the deep drift of cloud. The wind fell, for a second, round Thornfield; but far away over wood and water poured a wild, melancholy wail: it was sad to listen to, and I ran off again.

5.2 COMMENTARY

Chapter 23, in which Rochester proposes, ends with the chestnut being struck by lightning. Chapter 24 explores the tense nature of their relationship, but stops on an ominous note. Jane tells us that she 'could not, in those days, see God for His creature, of whom I had made an idol'. Both cast long shadows over the present chapter, which is a 'crisis' in the narrative in the traditional sense of a turning point in the story, and in the modern sense of something deeply wrong.

Chapter 25, with its crisis of the impending marriage, exemplifies the novel's characteristic of operating simultaneously on different narrative levels. As we see from the previous chapter, the marriage terms are not yet equal ones; Rochester still has a wish to dominate, while Jane, having made an idol of him, is apt to acquiesce. This inequality, and the inappropriateness of marrying under these conditions, is registered by Jane's instinctive refusal to recognise her new name and clothes, as these do not yet 'fit'. Her refusal to own herself as the Mrs Rochester denoted by the luggage label might merely reflect her anxiety that all goes well, which she does not want to jeopardise by counting her chickens before they hatch; but at a deeper level it helps signify that the Mrs Rochester envisioned by Rochester – an illusory figure identified with the fancy new clothes he has purchased for her – is a character deeply at odds with Jane's 'real' character, which she cannot put on without jeopardising her identity. Her wedding garments, moreover, give off a 'ghostly shimmer', a further hint that the 'Mrs Rochester' to be, is an illusion. Jane's feverish response to it suggests that it is also a dangerous, unsettling illusion, and so she flees outdoors, into tempestuous, but congenial nature.

The next paragraph gives Jane's commonsensical explanation for her anxiety, but her third reason – here held in abeyance – suggests that there are other, more mysterious reasons. As we eventually learn, they concern her strange dream, and upon waking, the appearance of the real Mrs Rochester, who rips her wedding veil in two. The holding back of this reason is essential to Charlotte Brontë's narrative technique, which is to create mystery, but also suspense; we are therefore more likely to scan the imagery that follows for the clues it offers.

The themes advanced by the narrative alert us that something is amiss, that the opposites Jane must juggle have not yet found their equipoise. The imagery of the paragraphs that follow helps us piece together how this might be so. The paragraph beginning, 'I sought the orchard', suggests a link between the internal and external, that Jane's inner state is mirrored in the weather, which is dark where it should be clear, and rising in restless ferocity. The next paragraph significantly tells us that Jane drew 'a certain wild pleasure' from running before the wind, with 'wild' darkly suggestive of intemperance. Earlier in the novel Rochester's initial response to Mason's appearance is likened to an oak being felled by lightning. The sundered chestnut might thereby signify Rochester, and later on the connection is explicitly made (Chapter 37). The imagery is therefore pointed: the tree has been cloven, but the trunk is entire, a partial damage that anticipates Rochester's, before Jane finds and restores him. Indeed, the speech of the succeeding paragraph could be directly applied to Rochester as he is in later life, while the 'adhesion at the faithful, honest roots', could be applied to the both of them, as they remain true despite the coming adversity. But the completion of these foreshadowings – which also tell on Jane's future plight – are still in the offing, so the suggestion arises that the image also pertains to Jane, and that she too is internally, but not irreparably, 'split'.

The final paragraph suggests how this could be so by hinting that her inner self is compromised by unchecked passion. As we have seen, the moon serves as an index of Jane's inner state, a bright full moon indicating Jane's proper, or ideal, condition. But here it is eclipsed by cloud, and is blood-red. The two images (moon and cloud) modify each other. Just as in the last chapter Rochester eclipses the sun, so the tumultuous clouds eclipse the moon. The blood-red colour of the moon signifies intemperate, obscuring passion (as it does for Rochester, who uses the same image in Chapter 27 to describe the sexual bafflement of his failed marriage). So Jane is split by the tension between physical and spiritual love, which leaves her as restless and feverish as the weather. The initial suggestion is that the narrative has reached a crisis owing to an imminent marriage where the 'sexual politics' are uneven; but we now see that it is also in crisis owing to Jane's internal divisions (which would link back to the preceding chapter's statement that Jane has made an idol of Rochester – that is to say, that her love is unbalanced).

The scene and imagery thus bear a range of possible meanings. Reading so much into the imagery may seem problematic, but this very richness is the source of the novel's attraction and power. Nor have we exhausted the fund of suggestion. For example, Jane says of the sundered tree that its 'time of pleasure and love is over'; the other things she says of the tree prove prophetically true, as regards herself and Rochester, but this opinion will later be contradicted by events. Rochester will love again; or is it suggesting that Jane's and Rochester's future love will be significantly different from the past?

Finally, one should note Jane's command of language, especially her ability to create rhythms that enhance her description while absorbing the reader. Jane's main technique is to alter the pace of her language through a judicious use of alliteration, rhyme, assonance, and patterned sentence structure.

For example, note how Jane's language changes in the course of the first paragraph. It starts ominously with Jane's double mention of time (the 'wasted' month and 'numbered' hours) emphasising time's worrying rush. 'Day' is then mentioned twice, which also hints at a dramatic menace. The language then becomes more briskly colloquial, creating a brightening, no-nonsense effect, as in 'there were my trunks, packed, locked, corded...' The prosaic atmosphere of the middle part of the paragraph continues with the homely details of the cards of address, and the relative absence of patterning which one associates with normal, unworried speech. But this changes when Jane describes the contents of the wardrobe, where her language becomes more 'musical'. For example, note the assonance and alliteration, the repetition of vowels and consonants in 'the pearl-coloured robe, the vapoury veil pendent from the usurped portmanteau. I shut the door to conceal the strange, wraith-like apparel it contained'. As Jane touches upon the 'mystery', or items involved in it, her language becomes more 'poetic', which both alters the pace of the narrative and increases the mystery through its eerie music. In this instance, the long 'o' in 'robe' and 'eau', and the 'a' in 'strange', 'vapour', 'veil' and 'contained', serve to slow the pace disconcertingly.

This alteration of tone and rhythm occurs throughout the specimen passage. Another device, a quickening one, is the use of syntactic repetition. For example, there is the parallelism of 'it seemed to augment its rush and deepen its roar'. There then follow three balanced verb phrases: 'the trees blew steadfastly one way, never writhing round, and scarcely tossing back'. A long phrase breaks the syntactic rhythm (although assonance and alliteration are still at work) before the triplicate structuring – the phrasing by threes – returns with the rhyming 'the clouds drifted from pole to pole, fast following, mass on mass'.

Usually the rhythm alters towards the end of the paragraph, with the next one breaking the spell. Twice this occurs with Jane addressing us directly, which allows her to switch her language back to the more measured, less ruffled rhythms of 'everyday' speech. The second paragraph is more cool, because more abstract (in that she explains what it is that makes her 'feverish'), while the third is prosaic because it describes Rochester away on business. So subject-matter, too, can effect a change of pace (although only in part). But as the paragraphs progress Jane turns towards description, telling us about the tree or the moon, and here once again the poetic rhythms gather.

If Jane used this more patterned language constantly, the effect would wear thin, but through her alteration of pace a sense of tension is created, as if Jane were trying to pull away into cool detachment, while another force worked to drag her into the atmosphere of the unnamed menace. Jane tells us that she feels 'feverish', but we would not be convinced without it being *dramatically* conveyed through her varied use of language. One can think of this variety as an alteration between 'rhetoric' and 'informal prose'. Rhetoric is the art of persuasion, and depends upon patterned language use (which can make it seem 'poetic'); informal prose avoids conspicuous patterning in order to seem 'natural'. To heighten the drama Jane thickens her rhetoric. In this respect Jane is not the naïve 'speaker' she may seem.

6 CRITICAL RECEPTION

6.1 CONTEMPORARY APPRAISALS

Jane Eyre provoked immediate acclaim, as well as a great deal of curiosity regarding the identity and sex of 'Currer Bell'. But two emerging issues proved of greater importance, as they set the agenda for much subsequent criticism: *Jane Eyre*'s 'coarseness', and the improbability of its plot.

Opinion was very much divided on these issues, although it must be said that even the hostile minority admitted the book's power. On the whole, opinion divided along establishment and liberal lines, the former execrating the book, the other praising it, although often with reservations. The most damning comments came from Elizabeth Rigby, in the *Quarterly Review* (1848), from which we quoted earlier (see Section 1.2). The book displayed an inexcusable 'coarseness of language and laxity of tone'; Jane Eyre's speech reveals her 'pedantry, stupidity, or gross vulgarity'. *The Christian Remembrancer*, of the same year, elaborates on this in a more 'sympathetic' way: 'There is an intimate acquaintance with the worst parts of human nature, a practised sagacity in discovering the latent ulcer, and a ruthless rigour in exposing it, which command our admiration.' *The Spectator* of the year before had joined in by saying the book was 'unnatural', 'artificial', and 'sordid'. These critics' distaste seems to have been at least partially motivated by differences in political outlook. Elizabeth Rigby complains that Jane is 'the personification of an unregenerate and undisciplined spirit' (the *Quarterly Review*). 'Every page burns with moral Jacobinism' was how *The Christian Remembrancer* made the political point (Jacobins being violent French revolutionaries).

Another source of distaste is here identified by one of Charlotte Brontë's shrewd French critics, Émile Montégut, who noted that it was quite unsurprising that Rochester's and Jane's amorous conversations should have shocked English sensibilities: 'they are as stifling as a hot summer day, as intoxicating as the exhalations of nature; they possess the mind like a contagion' (*Revue des Deux Mondes*, August 1857).

One of Charlotte Brontë's favourite reviews was written by another Frenchman, Eugène Forçade. The compliment Charlotte Brontë paid it makes it worth looking into: 'it is one of the most able . . . of any that has yet appeared. Eugène Forçade understood and enjoyed *Jane Eyre*.' Forçade begins his review by remarking on the calamitous nature of the 1848 revolution in Paris, a seminal event in European history. For him the dream of a socialist utopia, with its levelling tendencies, is 'the sickness of our time'. The principal weapon against this sickness is 'poetry', which glorifies 'the individual history of human emotion', an individualism which destroys the illusion of equality (*Revue des Deux Mondes*, October 1848). Forçade champions *Jane Eyre* as just such timely 'poetry'. We thus have the interesting paradox of Charlotte's English critic attacking *Jane Eyre* as seditious, whereas her French critic – in the midst of revolution – sees it as a bulwark against sedition. Belief in individualism, in self-reliance and self-help, was a central aspect of the middle-class outlook, one shared by Forçade. Forçade felt that socialism would lead to an absence of struggle, a dependence on the state, and a machine-like sameness in humanity. *Jane Eyre* therefore appeared anti-revolutionary because it glorified individual struggle and self-help. But self-help also implied social mobility, something the more establishment Rigby apparently found distasteful.

Charlotte Brontë's hostile critics charged her with having a gross, crude, and therefore unbelievable subject-matter. Her appreciative critics, who predominated, often praised the same subject-matter for being the reverse, G. H. Lewes saying that the book possessed a 'reality – deep, significant reality' (*Fraser's Magazine*, December 1847). But while her friendly critics were happy with the content, they were often worried by the extravagant plotting. The enthusiastic Forçade felt compelled to say that he could not fathom the need for 'such complicated and disjointed incidents, often improbably linked'. G. H. Lewes simultaneously complained of 'too much melodrama and improbability', while also inventing a formula that explained it: there is a 'faculty of objective representation . . . united to a strange power of subjective representation' (*Fraser's Magazine*, December 1847). Émile Montégut is once again extremely helpful: 'If men's purest dreams were discernible, it would generally be found that there was something equivocal about them. Now, *Jane Eyre* is a passionate dream.' He elaborates his argument by saying that he attaches 'little importance to certain glaring artificial details, certain melodramatic inventions, certain over-romantic combinations . . . these improbabilities are in my opinion much better motivated than has generally been acknowledged'. Montégut both defends the book's realism and locates its subjective, dreamy power; that is to say, besides the powerful naturalistic scenes, we have a telling 'dreamlike' symbolism with its equivocal messages, a fair enough gloss on Lewes's 'formula'.

One other contemporary comment deserves to be quoted for the way it concisely articulates much current interest in the book, and that is by Margaret Oliphant. She notes how the book 'defied the principles' of 'our well-ordered world'. Naturally readers were aghast to discover this 'grossness' to have been written by a woman. 'Nobody perceived that it was a new generation nailing its colours to its mast. No one would understand that this furious love-making was but a wild declaration of the "Rights of Woman" in a new aspect' (*Blackwood's Magazine*, May 1855).

6.2 RECENT APPRAISALS

Jane Eyre's melodrama, conventionality and incredible plotting continued to worry twentieth-century critics. Lord David Cecil, in his influential *Early Victorian Novelists* (1934), complained that the book was overly subjective, conventional, and too detached from its subject to create meaningful satire. 'Formless, improbable, humourless' though the book was, it was still to be seen as the work of a powerful 'creative imagination' – in other words as a triumph of untutored nature over art. The dominant critical approach at this time was the New Criticism, which rested on the belief that a work of art should have a content fully integrated with its form; thus the work should be aesthetically 'seamless'. With its unregulated anger and creaking coincidences, *Jane Eyre* seemed anything but, and those anxious to defend the book either took recourse in the 'freak genius' account favoured by Lord Cecil, or sought to extricate a hidden unity by focusing on the book's symbolic pattern, or by revealing the accomplished way Charlotte Brontë modified Gothic melodrama. A further consequence of the New Critical approach was that *Jane Eyre* was seen to suffer badly in comparison with the work of her sister, Emily, an unsurprising development as almost any novel would suffer in comparison with the extraordinary *Wuthering Heights*. The recent upsurge in feminist criticism has tended to redress this by changing the basis of comparison, not asking 'which is the most unified work of art?', but 'what does each novel say regarding the lives of mid-Victorian women?' Critical trends apart, *Jane Eyre* has had a secure, unwavering place in the public's affection ever since it was first published.

REVISION QUESTIONS

1. According to Matthew Arnold, Charlotte Brontë's mind contained 'nothing but hunger, rebellion, and rage', and this disfigured her work. Is this true of *Jane Eyre*?
2. Do you agree with Margaret Oliphant's view that *Jane Eyre* represented a 'declaration of the "Rights of Woman" '?
3. Discuss the contribution the minor characters make to an understanding of the novel.
4. Elizabeth Rigby believed *Jane Eyre* to be radical, whereas Eugène Forçade saw it as a 'protest against socialism'. With whom do you agree?
5. How helpful is it to see Helen Burns and Mrs Rochester as Jane's *alter egos*?
6. 'Jane's and Rochester's conversations reveal a shifting balance of power, and by the end of the novel Jane has adopted the "masculine" or dominant role, Rochester the "feminine" or submissive one.' Do you agree?
7. Analyse the novel's references to nature and grace.
8. What are *Jane Eyre*'s most important symbols, and what do they contribute to an understanding of the novel?
9. Can we believe Jane when she tells us that she was right when she 'adhered to principle and law', and scorned the temptation to go with Rochester to the South of France? Is she here, and elsewhere, a reliable narrator?
10. Is the improbability of *Jane Eyre*'s plot a fault?
11. Are Jane Eyre's attitudes towards class consistent?
12. What do the scenes involving Brocklehurst add to an understanding of the novel?
13. Does Rochester ever pose a threat to Jane? If so, how?
14. What is the purpose of the episode in the red-room?
15. 'The child is mother to the woman.' To what extent is this true of Jane Eyre?

16. If *Jane Eyre* is a 'novel of education', what is it that Jane learns?
17. Does *Jane Eyre* employ the 'romance' form critically, or is it essentially 'escapist' in tendency?
18. Consider Charlotte Brontë's use of the first person narrator and the significance it has for our understanding of the book.

FURTHER READING

Elaine Showalter's *A Literature of Their Own: British Women Novelists from Brontë to Lessing* (Virago, 1982), Eva Figes's *Sex and Subterfuge: Women Writers to 1850* (Macmillan, 1982), and Sandra Gilbert and Susan Gubar's *The Madwoman in The Attic: the Woman Writer and the Nineteenth-Century Literary Imagination* (Yale University Press, 1979) all contain interesting readings of *Jane Eyre* from a feminist perspective. Eva Figes is particularly recommended for her account of the Gothic novel, while Cora Ann Howells's *Love, Mystery and Misery: Feeling in Gothic Fiction* (The Athlone Press, 1978) interprets *Jane Eyre* in the light of the Gothic tradition. Terry Eagleton's *Myths of Power: A Marxist Study of the Brontës* (Macmillan, 1975) interestingly reads *Jane Eyre* as an attempt at reconciling 'bourgeois initiative and genteel settlement, sober rationality and Romantic passion, spiritual equality and social distinction, the actively affirmative and the patiently deferential self'. Tom Winnifrith's *The Brontës and their Background: Romance and Reality* (Macmillan, 1973) offers an extremely useful commentary on the Brontës' religion and contemporary sexual mores. *The Brontës: the Critical Heritage*, edited by Miriam Allott (Routledge & Kegan Paul, 1973) contains an absorbing selection of contemporary reviews. Much of the same material is available in *Charlotte Brontë,* Jane Eyre *and* Villette: *A Casebook* (Macmillan, 1973), also edited by Miriam Allott but supplemented by helpful selections typifying the New Critical debate. Margot Peters's *Unquiet Soul* (Hodder & Stoughton, 1975) is the first avowedly 'feminist' biography, while Phyllis Bentley's *The Brontës and Their World* (Thames & Hudson, 1974) succinctly and atmospherically tells the life with the aid of documents and pictures. The first, and still most celebrated, biography was written by Mrs Gaskell (1857), who was Charlotte Brontë's friend in later life.